WRITING ART AND ARCHITECTURE

TRANSMISSION

Transmission denotes the transfer of information, objects or forces from one place to another, from one person to another. Transmission implies urgency, even emergency: a line humming, an alarm sounding, a messenger bearing news. Through Transmission interventions are supported, and opinions overturned. Transmission republishes classic works in philosophy, as it publishes works that re-examine classical philosophical thought. Transmission is the name for what takes place.

WRITING ART AND ARCHITECTURE

Andrew Benjamin

re.press Melbourne 2010

re.press

PO Box 40, Prahran, 3181, Melbourne, Australia
http://www.re-press.org

British Library Cataloguing-in-Publication Data
A catalogue record for this book is available from the British Library

Library of Congress Cataloguing-in-Publication Data
A catalogue record for this book is available from the Library of Congress

National Library of Australia Cataloguing-in-Publication Data

Benjamin, Andrew E
Writing art and architecture / Andrew E. Benjamin.

9780980668360 (pbk. with colour images)
9780980819700 (pbk. with b&w images)
9780980668377 (ebook)

Series: Transmission.
Subjects: Aesthetics.
Architecture.
Art.
Writing.

700.1

Designed and Typeset by *A&R*

This book is produced sustainably using plantation timber, and printed in the destination market reducing wastage and excess transport.

CONTENTS

LIST OF PLATES

ACKNOWLEDGEMENTS

These essays were written with the support of editors, colleagues, students and friends. The practice of criticism necessitates committed publishers. While these essays stem from a number of publications a significant number were written for *Architectural Review Australia*. As such I would like to acknowledge my editors there—Mat Ward and Andrew Mackenzie—who were and remain enormously supportive. I would like to thank the artists who invited me to write on their work. While rewritten these texts first appeared, for the most part, as catalogue essays.

'Performing, Effecting Surfaces' first appeared in Dagmar Richter, *Armed Surfaces*, Black Dog Publishing, London, 2004; 'Vandalizing Objects' in *Art Monthly* (no. 163, september 2003); 'Architecture and Culture' in *Architecture Australia* (vol. 92. no. 3 May/June 2003); 'Fraying Lines' in Richard Goodwin's *Richard Goodwin: Performance to Porosity (2006)*. The following all appeared in *Architectural Review Australia*: 'The Standards of the Non Standard' (no. 87), 'Displaying Architecture' (no. 92), 'Architecture as Practice' (no. 94), 'On the Library' (no. 100), 'Learning From the House' (no. 101), 'Myth and History' (no. 102), 'Serra and the Space of Sculpture' (no. 103), 'Reflections on Architectural Theory' (no. 106) and 'Seeing Florence' (no. 108).

INTRODUCTION

WRITING, CRITICISM
Art, Architecture

Writing about art and architecture occurs in many guises. While there will always be a connection between historical and critical understandings the writings presented here are for the most part acts of criticism. Criticism, however, cannot be reduced to the location or even the attribution of value. Criticism has a different register. It works in a different way.

At its most straightforward criticism involves the identification of art and architecture. However, identification is not just the naming of works. On the contrary, identification concerns a more nuanced sense of identity. Allowing for a form of identification that cannot be equated either with the mere naming of a work or its description repositions criticism. As a result criticism is delimited by questions concerning how specific works work as either art or architecture. This doubling of 'work' is important. Too often art works and works of architecture are attributed a static quality. As if they were no more than documents, evidence or examples. If such a conception of work were allowed to predominate then what would be precluded, almost by definition, would have been any direct interest in the work's material presence or in the complex process of how works acquired material presence. The presence of materials and the process by which works are materialized—i.e. how they acquire material presence—is central precisely because the meaning of a work is always an after effect of the way materials operate. This will differ in regards to art and architecture, and within art between painting, sculpture and video—nonetheless, as a generalization, meaning cannot be (perhaps should not be) divorced from the work of materials. If this were to occur then allowing interpretive concerns to predominate as though the works in questions did not have an original relation to the broad question of materiality would be to idealize work. It would be as though meanings were just there, as though they had an evanescent relation to the materiality of the object. Integral to these writings is the supposition that criticism has a necessary relation to what could be described as a materialist aesthetics.

Once matter is attributed centrality then not only will this have an effect of how works are construed, it will also necessitates both the invention of a vocabulary as well as the transformation of pre-existing terms. However, neither inventions nor transformation are real if they are understood as the mere positing of a new set of terms. Such a move would restrict the new by equating it, even if only implicitly, with novelty. Transformation has a link to how materials are set to work. This sense of transformation occurs in two different though interrelated ways. In the first instance transformations are already present within works, or they are generated by the contemporary nature of work in a way that has retrospective force. If there is a sense of transformation whose location is brought out in the majority of these writings, then it stems from the consequences of the incorporation of the computer into the design process. This has given rise to a radical shift in how works—in the broadest sense of the term—are produced and therefore there is the concomitant need to reconsider how they are to be interpreted. Works occur today within an era of digital reproducibility. This specific site of production demands the production of concepts and categories that contemporary work necessitates.

The second sense of transformation can be linked to the performative dimension of particular works. Here this involves the relationship to traditions. Be it a relation to the tradition of housing or memorialization or modes of production within the visual arts transformation involves a repositioning of the tradition. Repositioning rather than abandoning of the given. Transformation, in this sense, occurs within works that *dis-order.* Equally, it can be traced in what has been described as the *fraying* of pre-established borders and divisions. Both these terms tie transformation and production together. Precisely, because of the retention of a sense of production—production as a generative process rather than an instrumental one—one of the additional key operative terms at work within these writings is *potentiality.* Diagrams, lines and surfaces within contemporary architecture are to be understood in terms of their potentiality. Their potentiality stems from what defines their presence as contemporary. They are the result of the transformation of the line and the surface within the era of digital reproducibility.

The writings presented had their initial publication within magazines, books and catalogues. Some were excised from a journal. All are experiments. They should be understood therefore as attempts within a defined and delimited space to engage with works. At times it is the work itself that is important. Either a work of architecture or particular paintings or sculptures. In every instance what is central is particularity and therefore the question of the way a given work works. There is however a twofold risk that attends any insistence on particularity. The first element is the equation of criticism with description. The second is the supposition that any writing on art or architecture is automatically criticism. Avoiding these two possibilities necessitates developing a specific understanding of particularity. The particular work is a material event. However, it is also incorporated within a network of relations. Material events—paintings, sculptures, buildings, etc.—recall, of necessity, the genre of which they form a part. Events acknowledge that relation even though they are not determined by it. Criticism, precisely because it is concerned with the way a work works—for example, the way in which a work works as sculpture or painting or an act of memorialization—locates the material event within that act of recall. What matters is the work. The work's mattering—matter as an active principle—is the interplay between material specificity and the network relations that become a given works own specific act of recall. Neither that network nor the work's mattering can be excluded. Their interplay is the object of criticism. However, that object is always particular. Neither a particular that stands alone, nor a particular that is determined by a form of universality. Rather the particular as a material event.

An important component of these writings is the exhibition, specifically the exhibition of architecture. Exhibitions are never neutral. What they always involve is the display of a conception of what architecture is taken to be. To that extent an exhibition is always a response to the question of criticism. That question concerns how works work as architecture and therefore the way materials and programme interconnect in the creation of the work as a material event. Consequently, the decision of what to display and how to display it has to be understood as a response to the question of how, in a given instance, the material event is being understood. Responding to the exhibition of architecture is a critical response to that understanding. There is, however, an additional element. The architectural exhibition recalls the fact that the history of architecture is inextricably bound up with practice of representation. Architecture cannot be divorced from the technical means of representation. Drawings, models and now computer generated diagrams form an essential part of that history. Understanding hat history and therefore working with the display of architecture has to acknowledge that history. What that acknowledgment means is working with the recognition that the digital now plays an essential role within the practice of design and therefore will also figure in the critical response to architecture's own self-presentation. The ubiquity of the digital gives rise to another way of understanding questions concerning representation in general, the relationship between the digital and the material and thus the display of architecture in general. Accepting this as the setting for the exhibition forms an important part of any critical response to specific exhibitions.

To suggest that these writings are experiments is to say that they are continual attempts to define and enact the project of criticism. They are therefore a form of practice. Criticism as a practice is of course distinct from the practices around which its own project is orientated. In fact it is a connection that is also disjunctive. This complex sense of location marks out the particularity of criticism while at the same time positioning this mode of writing as experimental. Criticism cannot close the opening between writing and its object. However, the fact that closure is impossible and that it cannot complete the object generates a form of responsibility. The responsibility is to maintain the object as a material event. If it is conceded that this is the only way to maintain particularity then any other approach—description, mere historicization, subjective response, etc.—will in the end efface what is specific to a particular work. Particularity does not just emerge within the activity of criticism, criticism as a practice sustains it.

ARCHITECTURE + DESIGN

ARCHITECTURE AND CULTURE

Opening

Perhaps the most well known line from Adolf Loos's famous essay: 'Ornament and Crime' is the claim that, '[a]s ornament is no longer organically related to our culture, it is also no longer the expression of our culture'. This move, which separates ornament and culture, links modernist architecture to the culture of modernity. As with any link it can be as much championed as disavowed. Nonetheless, two things emerge. The first is a statement of intent. The second is a question. In the first instance, and unavoidably, modernist architecture defines itself in relation to culture. The definition is clear. And yet, despite this definition, the question of how today that relation is to be understood has a persistent quality that is usually noticed in its occlusion. In other words, to the extent that the link is denied, and that architecture is seen as no more than building and thus thought in terms of a differentiation of the economic from the cultural, the possible presence of architecture's relation to culture emerges as a question whose acuity cannot be readily escaped. What then is architecture's relation to culture?

In purely strategic terms the question has relevance since policy—usually in terms of Government policy and even architectural criticism—often uses straightforwardly economic criteria to make decisions or draw conclusions. Approaching architecture as an industry, while apposite in certain instances, fails to allow for the presence of the architectural to form part of a nation's, or a community's, culture. And yet, it is clear that the presence of architecture in the daily lives of citizens only underscores its ineliminable cultural presence. The task here is to address that presence and then draw conclusions that could have relevance as much for policy directed decisions, as it would for evaluative ones. Prompting this essay was not just the refusal of public money to the Australian pavilion at the 2004 Venice Biennale, but the need to engage with the issues to which such a refusal gives rise.[1] For the most part, the issues do not pertain to the relative strength or weakness of Australian architecture but to the way in which it defined itself. While there is no one self-definition there is a prevailing perception. Countering that perception and therefore reopening the need to link architecture to the wider world of policy—policy other than simple planning regulations—involves reopening the question of architecture's relation to culture.

Within the range of this essay there are two senses in which the word 'culture' will be used. The first relates to the activities that are often taken as specific to architecture. The other is inextricably connected to the realm of human existence. In respect to the latter what it demarcates are the ways in which human life relates itself to 'nature'. While there may be two different senses of the word culture what matters is the way concerns of one can be—perhaps should be—intruded into the other. There is little point holding to the exclusivity of the culture of architecture as this denies its presence as part of human society. Equally, architecture cannot be thought as nothing other than merely cultural as this would preclude any consideration being given, for example, to the way different materials realize different effects within architectural practice.

The way through this complex set of considerations will result from recognizing that these two different senses of culture are interrelated. Insisting on that interrelation introduces another defining element into the equation. Indeed, it marks the point of relation: namely, the public. Architecture is essentially public. While this is hardly a surprising claim since it seems to be true by definition. As with many truths the acceptance of what it asserts is conterminous with the refusal of its consequences. A choice emerges: Architecture can take the construction of objects that are positioned as only ever private and thus which only open up the already circumscribed worlds of individual activity—e.g. the domestic house—as that which defines its sphere of operation. Or, there

1. In response to this exclusion a Virtual Australian Pavilion was created and exhibited on line for the 2004 Biennale. The exhibition was designed by John Gollings, Tom Kovac and David Pidgeon. The exhibition was curated by me. I have discussed some of the issues raised by the 2002 Biennale in 'What Next? Notes on the Venice Biennale', *Architecture Australia*, January/February 2003.

can be an insistence on its inherently public nature. Emphasizing the public does not mean that the construction of the house is in some sense a denial of that self-defined location. Rather, the argument would be that architecture's continual opening onto the world—an opening which can have an important role in the construction of that world—is one of the main ways for there to be a possible nexus between the culture of architecture and the inherently public nature of human sociality. What have to be explained therefore are the differences between these two positions.

This distinction is not between architecture as an academic activity on the one hand and as a worldly activity on the other. At work here are different conceptions of practice. The difference is crucial since in both instances there can be a championing of materials over programme; in both, a concern with the environmental consequences of building can be paramount; equally, issues pertaining to sustainability can drive them both. The distinction involves the extent to which there is an affirmation—with all the difficulties and complexities that this term brings with it—of the inherently public nature of architecture.

Opening In

Architecture can be described as *opening in*, when it defines itself in terms of an activity of construction for individuals to suit individual needs. In working from the outside in, space is created that reproduces the desires of clients. In so doing, that world takes on the veneer of the private. The privacy in question has a public register. However, that registration is of a conception of the private as the world in which the individual—either singularly or as a unit—has primacy. Moreover, it generates a conception of the public, as a collection of individuals all of whom aspire to the creation of their own 'private' world, which in being created would then be the locus where their own unique desires would be satisfied.

Architecture begins to define itself in these terms when this conception of practice—and world creation—becomes the basis for future discussions and evaluations. Once the object is understood as created for the individual, bringing with it a conception of the public as the totality of individuals, it follows that architecture is both the expression of personalities, and that the built object expresses the personality of the client. (Or at least that this would be the desired intent on both sides.) Equally, because construction, once understood in this light is always defined by a conception of individual taste, there cannot be a link to a conception of culture other than one arising from a generalization of the individual. It is not difficult to imagine that once this is accepted as the definition of architecture—and it will be a self-definition that will work at a range of different scales—architecture will be inevitably understood as a series of produced (built, constructed, etc.) objects that are created by individuals to serve individual ends. Since the public is always counter posed to the individual, and this will be true even when the public is understood as the abstract presence of the totality of individuals, architecture will be defined in terms of singular relations. The relation is always between architect and client. Architecture remains enclosed within that relation. What is important is the extent to which that relation is taken to define the practice.

Once there is a turning towards the interior then there is no need to think in terms of the registration of the exterior. Those elements—minimally the exterior to which architecture opens out—will pertain to culture understood as part of the public domain. The limit of the self-definition does not have to do with a specific program—though it should be added that the preconceived preoccupation of Australian architecture with domestic housing only exacerbates the situation. The insistence of the interior, and a self-definition that defines architecture in terms of individual concerns—and reciprocally as only of concern for individuals—means that it is a simple matter to locate architecture as no more than an economic activity. The construction of a house would have a bespoke suit as its correlate. The refusal of the public is, of course, a positioned relation to the inherently public nature of architecture. Not only does this establish the limit of architecture's self definition in terms of what has been described as *opening in*; it also indicates that the culture of architecture is from the start traversed by the complex matter of culture.

The already present place of culture needs to be noted. Here, it concerns the capacity for an object to stage a relation. While this may seem an overly complex point it is not. Staging is not just the presence of program nor is it just the use of one combination of materials rather than another. Staging becomes the way the interarticulation of a program and materials work to present a specific conception of the program in question. Within these terms architecture becomes a material event. The differences, for example, between two museums are to be found in terms of what they stage. That is, the way the understanding or self-conception of the programme, the geometry proper to its realization, and the materials, once combined yield the object as a material event. However, it is an object as a site of activity. The activity is the way the building stages its presence. Two things need to be noted here. The first is that staging is integral to the way in which an object works as architecture. The second is that programme, geometry, and the use of materials have both a historical and cultural dimension. What this means is that staging necessarily inscribes boarder cultural considerations into the integrity of the architectural object. *Opening in*, therefore, becomes the attempt to avoid defining architecture in terms of that inscription. The counter—*opening out*—becomes the way of acknowledging the insistent presence of staging and of allowing that acknowledgment to play a pivotal role in establishing architecture's self-definition

Opening Out

Emphasizing, both that architecture is from the start a staging, and that part of such a self-definition is an explicit acknowledgement of architecture's public nature, does not mean that henceforth architecture has to be either utilitarian—i.e. merely functional—or instrumental—i.e. driven by some large social goal. Moreover, there will not just be one way in that such an acknowledgment need be present. The complex surfaces of the Online Multimedia Centre, at the St Albans campus of Victoria University by Lyons, for example, opens up a potential urban field. This does not occur by locating the architecture on the surface, but by allowing the surface to aid in creating a visual urbanism. What emerges, as much as a potential than as that which is actually realized, are urban surfaces. The interest in the surface as evinced by Lyons—and here there is an important affinity with some recent work by Herzog and de Meuron, in particular their library for the Eberswalde Polytechnic—should be understood as locating the object's architecture as much in a sustained engagement with programmatic concerns, as it is in the construction of urban surfaces. The importance of the latter is that they take the creation of surfaces beyond any concern with the decorative.

While a great deal has been written about ARM's National Museum in Canberra, it remains the case that its singular importance lies in the specific way it stages a conception of the public and thus of community. While it enhances the site, to argue that a building compliments Walter Burly Griffen's master plan runs the risk of condemning it in advance. At the National Museum identity becomes a site of endless negotiation and the symbols carry that positioning. Both work together to define the site. Rather than concentrate on the symbols *per se*, what is actually fundamental to their presence is that they introduce a conception of time that is not determined by immediacy. The symbols stage a more complex and always to-be-determined conception of identity. There is still a connection between symbols and symbolized, however, what needs to be noted is that the link is hard to establish as definitive. Indeed that is the point. The public nature of the architecture, and in addition its democratic impulse, are to be found in the symbolism because the work attests to the complex and cosmopolitan nature of the public. While a fundamentally different project LAB's Federation Square demands, amongst other things, that reconsideration be given to how, within the urban context figure/ground relations have to be recast in terms of figure/figure relations. The inscription of an implicit urbanism into The Ian Potter Centre at the National Gallery of Victoria, the construction of the Squares themselves as having an explicit urbanism, the complex relation that both have to the urbanism created by the intersections of the grid and the lanes, fed by public transport hubs means that each element becomes an important figure constructing the urban terrain.[2] While it does not occur literally, Federation Square develops—both externally and internally (i.e. within the Ian Potter Centre itself)—the urbanism of its setting, while demanding a rethinking of how interventions of this scale within a pre-existing fabric are to be understood.

The significance of these projects cannot be understood in terms of the image they project. In other words, it is not as though subsequent work—be it large scale or the domestic house—has to have a Lyons' surface, or deploy complex symbolism, or enact fractal geometries. The fact of their significance does not mean that they set the measure for what architecture has to look like. It is not a question of appearance. Rather, what has to occur is a process of abstraction where what characterizes them—and it will always be the interplay of the strictly architectural and the cultural, one figuring in the other—is allowed to set the framework in which

2. I have discussed the aspect of Federation Square in my *Style and Time: Essays on the Politics of Appearance*, Northwestern University Press, Chicago, 2006, pp. 99-105.

architecture's self-definition can continue to be developed. Such a move by affirming the presence of the cultural—by noting the ineliminability of the public, while allowing both to have a complex and contested status—continues to allow for architecture to be opened up beyond any reduction. Be that reduction one to the simply economic or to the merely cultural, it goes without saying that such a position is necessarily contestable. Moreover, this inherent contestability may result in the refusal of the interplay of cultures and therefore in the championing of the interdependence of the private and the economic. The victory of one over the other reveals an essential truth. Namely, that the presence of the conflict—the inescapable hold of contestability—is the first step in any argument for the inherently cultural nature of the architectural.

ON THE LIBRARY
Reading and Writing in Public

The library houses. To think, however, that the problematic of the house provides a way into the library—as though all that is really at stake is the provision of public lounge rooms—is to fail grasp the increasing complex relation between public and private space in which the library needs to be located. Equally, libraries are at the forefront of any concern with the archive and thus the process of archivization. The relationship between, for example, a national historical collection of documents and books and their subsequent digital storage and use necessitates that this aspect of the library be reconsidered. This reconsideration will be as much curatorial as architectural.

Approaching the library therefore demands that what predominates are questions of public space on the one hand and the nature of the archive on the other. These two domains should overlap productively within the process of design. Making this claim is not to assert that the design process takes them into consideration. The argument is simply that noting their centrality constructs what might be described as a field in which judgment become possible.

The public used to be identified with the national. In that context public space became the domain in which the national was staged. Pelçnik's National University Library in Ljubljana (1941), for example, was an attempt to integrate a conception of Slovenian identity with a specific conception of modernity.[3] After Pleçnik the relationship between national identity or even local identity and the architectural no longer has a determining role in the how the library is designed, let alone in how it appears. Indeed, it is

3. I have taken up this aspect of Pelçnik's library in *Style and Time*, pp. 84-89.

possible to conjecture that while there is a recidivist conception of nationhood that continues to show itself in populist political discourses, any real engagement with the politics of public space knows from the start that neither the public let alone public architecture can be defined in ways that conflate or identify the public with an essentialist sense of national identity. In the context of Pleçnik's project, the public is conflated with the national. If this move is no longer possible, how is public space to be understood?

Any response to this question and thus any attempt to create public space have to take a diverse sense of the public into consideration. That diversity has an effect on how space is conceptualized. Equally, however, public space is a locus of control. Security guards and CCTV define public space in terms of monitoring. Public space cannot be conceived outside its assumed relation to question of policing. That there may be a tension between policing and the diversity that defines the public, a diversity that reworks the public in terms of the cosmopolitan, has to be acknowledged as a given. Design cannot resolve the conditions that generate it, nonetheless, the practice of design has to register its presence. What then of public concerns?

Another way in is needed. Indeed, the answer to this question resides in a reconsideration of the archive. The library's relation to storage is ubiquitous. Libraries are repositories. They are sites in which material is deployed and used, creating and recreating national and international narrative constructions, reconstructing lives, projecting possibilities and undoing already determined histories. Archives hold possibilities. They are sites of potentiality. Traditionally, access to the archive works through a hierarchy. Such a structure has its inevitable set of protocols. With the assumed centrality of material objects the hierarchy will have a structure that is determined by the materiality of the object and the role of the objects within already existing historical, national and regional narratives. A clear example is SOM's Beinecke Library at Yale University which was built for the maintenance and celebration of rare books and manuscripts.

With the material object, access will always need to be policed in a number of different ways such that filters begin to limit approaches to the books and manuscripts. At each level there will be further forms of restriction. At work is a gradation of access. It is not too difficult to envisage that such a programmatic imperative will have a direct impact on design.

While the digitalization of the archive does not resolve the question of storage, nor does it eliminate a hierarchy of access, what it does achieve is a radical reconfiguration of that process. Digitalization operates in a number of different ways. Collections of documents and manuscripts can be stored digitally. Books and journals can be accessed digitally. Databases allow for searches that extend beyond the material confines of the building. The corpus of entire literatures can be stored digitally. (This has already occurred with the body of work in Ancient Greek and Latin.) Images, representing the majority holding of museums, are increasingly at hand. The screen therefore becomes a site in which material can be employed that reaches within the building whilst reaching outside.

It should not be thought that the impact of the digital on the library involves the move from material presence to digital presence. Such a description is too simplistic. What is reconfigured in the process is the reading, the writing that stems from it, and more significantly the status of the reader. This reconsideration is enacted within the library. However, it no longer has to be a relationship between the reader and the process of reading and writing that was structured by the same hieratical process that defined the relation when centrality had to be attributed to the materiality of the book or the document. Or, where the materials (the read) were defined exclusively by their location in the library.

Through the process of digitization the assumed difference between the archive and the open collection is more nuanced. While the archive necessitates storage, and while there is always the need for originals to be consulted, the nature of that need is subject to change. Moreover, the readers accessing rare and precious documents and books no longer occupy an already defined category. As a result the question of the reader—of who is able to read and thus who has the right to access—will have been posed in an importantly different way. If there is a parallel situation then this opening has its correlate in the potentiality that the archive—in the broadest sense of the term—will have always contained.

In this regard it is significant that Terroir's competition entry for the New National Library of the Czech Republic (2007) uses the presence of the actual archive as a structuring device within their design. Refusing to conflate the archive with mere storage they conceive a different relation. The archive is defined by its potentiality. The archive therefore is neither literal presence nor is it mere metaphor. The archive which would be located within the terrain's folds is envisaged to work up through the building interrupting predetermined spatial arrangements. Part of the work would be the construction of public spaces. In so doing, the archive as a reality as well as an architectural concept has a material and thus a tectonic effect.

Once the archive is defined by potentiality then it accords with a conception of the public in which the latter is no longer equated with a forced homogeneity in which hierarchies are naturalized. The public becomes a locus of diversity and the cosmopolitan. It is therefore a collectivity whose actions cannot be regulated in advance. Hence, public space is its own archive. If there is a way of negotiating the presence of policing then it has to do with the recognition that the policing that hinders experimentation operates within structures which contain and limit the given. What cannot be policed is potentiality. The digitalization of the archive and thus its emergence as an open structure defined by infinite use coupled to a conception of the public and public space defined in terms of a potentially unmasterable diversity should reposition the library. A repositioning that will demand a different response to the question of what it means to read and write in public.

LEARNING FROM THE HOUSE

Architecture learns. Indeed there may be an imperative that it so do. Perhaps the most significant moment announcing this need occurs in the opening of Venturi and Scott Brown's *Leaning from Las Vegas*. 'Learning from the existing landscape is a way of being revolutionary in architecture'. Learning becomes for them a way of looking. Leaning and looking are interconnected. That interconnection gives centrality to the given. In their project learning and looking involved specific building types. Nonetheless, it took the urban as its point of departure. More significantly looking was defined by a body that moved. No longer static or positioned within the conventions of the perspectival sketch, *Learning from Las Vegas* linked movement and looking and thus introduced a connection between sight and speed. Any attempt to answer the questioning whether architecture can still learn can only ever be specific. Here the point of departure is the more localized question: What would it mean for architecture to learn from the house?

Answering this question necessitates a type of return. Returning to the house must occur in ways that are stripped of any innocence. Houses house. The question to be addressed is what defines the activity, Housing, understood as an activity, continues to take place. Precisely because of that continuity the question of definition cannot be given by a simple recourse to detail. Definition demands the recognition that the house is from the start a structuring of domestic space and as such an enacting of the porous divide between the public and private. The terms 'domestic', 'public' and 'private' are all central.

While the meaning of each term is thought to be obvious the situation is inherently more complex. To the extent that the domestic is defined by its equation with the private, then the domestic is always positioned by acts of separation. If however the domestic is defined by its relation to public space, then a different situation occurs. Rather than modes of separation the lines demarcating and structuring urban space can be drawn through the domestic defining and therefore redefining both site and programmatic organization. While this definition, thus measure, is inevitable, what matters is what provides it.

The history of the house would seem to correspond to the move from a concern with the public to the private such that the urban nature of the domestic architecture cedes its place to the disclosure of an internal world. However, the interruption of this development cannot occur by simply insisting that the continuity of the equation of the domestic with private ought not occur and that all architecture should engage with its inherently public nature. (And this no matter how much that nature may have been muted or even effaced.) There needs to be a different argument. Architecture can learn little from the reduction of the house to detail. All that could be gained from such an equation is the presence of certain houses as exemplary. Were they to instruct it would be in relation to images of their actual presence. Learning would have become edification. Holding back this possibility means that the house should have a different inflection.

Learning from what is at hand cannot involve the mere repetition of what is already there. Learning involves abstraction. More emphatically it necessitates abstraction. The way in which it is possible learn from the house therefore involves a transformation. As has already been noted the house is caught between forms of definition. Allowing for the urban to set the measure means moving the emphasis away from seeing the house as an exemplary instance of the domestic. If there is another way of looking then the literal cedes its place to a version abstraction. Abstractions have potentiality.

Abstraction opens in a number of different directions. In the case of Adolf Loos' Haus Müller or Rem Koolhaas' Bordeaux House an insistence on historical particularity, while important in certain instances, limits the house. The limit is the hold of history. However, to insist on their exemplarity status also limits them. They become single instances of a general type; instances from which little could be learned. However, once there is a process of transformation—a transformation in which abstraction predominates—then they become specific ways in which circulation defines bodily presence and materials cannot be thought other than in their relation to programme. Moreover, in the case of both these houses, even though the modes of circulation are importantly different, there is the interrelationship between movement, (and therefore the body) materials and programme. One cannot be thought without the other. In Haus Müller cladding is fundamental. In the Bordeaux House it is the use of an elementary palette of materials. In both instances the interconnection with circulation allows programme.

Rather than use a form of citation in which elements of preexiting architectural possibilities are noted—learning is not quotation—the possibilities inherent in these houses can only emerge when their description becomes abstract. Learning from Haus Müller would not involve the mere repetition of Loos. Learning occurs when there is a repetition that is given a form that has not occurred before. The repetition would not have been of the house's literal presence but of its presence as an abstraction. Learning therefore needs to be distinguished from imitation. Imitation is structured by representation. Learning however demands the move from abstraction to production; a move that depends upon abstraction's potentiality.

Abstraction becomes therefore a site open to inflection. The given is retained within the process of its transformation. Not only does the question of production remain open only if the house is positioned in these terms, both the literal reiteration of given building types as well as utopian speculation are effectively distanced. The given is looked at in way that allows for production. The presence of abstraction can also be present purely on the level of drawing. A number of Eisenman's early house projects are investigations of models of spatial transformation. As such they are indifferent to the question of materials. (Hence their difference from the concerns of Loos and Koolhaas.) Nonetheless, Eisenman's drawings have the potentiality to be viewed beyond any immediate reduction to representation and therefore as projective.

There are of course different modalities of inflection. Amounting to differing ways of account for forms of production, (thus different construals of design.) The inflection that merely picks up detail stills the potentiality of abstraction by turning the founding relations into a literal image. If the inflection maintains abstraction the question is always going to be how to avoid turning the abstract into the literal. In other words, how is the potential of abstraction to be maintained? One clear response is to move the concerns of the urban through the founding site of abstract relations. This is not a visual question. On the contrary it involves the interconnection between the public, the semi-public and what could be called the becoming-private of programmes within apartments blocks. Urban infrastructure, especially when it concerns forms of movement—from walking to public transport—should also inflect the site. Differing lines would intersect beginning to define the site while opening up a range of design strategies. The site need not become an image of the urban. The site would itself be inflected by elements of the urban's own abstract presence.

The house, of course, can be equally inflected. The limitations of that inflection are no more that the limits of the house itself. Nonetheless, each house has to negotiate its relation to the street. Equally it must enact the moment of becoming-private. In every instance the negotiation and the enactment can allow the urban to define the sites. Lines will work though the site rather than being closed off at the entrance. To the extent that the house can continue to be positioned in this way it eschews an identification of architecture with detail, thus learning from the house will be a real possibility.

PLUS ÇA CHANGE, PLUS ÇA CHANGE
Reflections on Architectural Theory

1.

One of the most exacting lessons that comes from any attempt to present a materialist account of the operation of a discipline within design is that the process, no matter how construed, cannot escape from the need to account both for the ways its practice is instantiated and the historical moment in which that practice is located.[4] In regard to practice the claim is not that a design practice results in actual designs. That would be a simple tautology. The claim is that the process of design necessitates the tools and implements that allow design to occur. The mechanisms of design cannot serve as predictors. However, were it not for their presence design could not occur at all. What occurs, what drives the differing modes of that occurrence, are both the techniques of its practice and the setting—both institutional and historical—that maintain it.

The role of theory with design education, specifically architectural theory within schools of architecture, has until quite recently flourished. Over the last thirty years the works of philosophers, anthropologists, and literary critics amongst others were deployed in order to animate the design process. In retrospect the flourishing of theory accompanied one of the most pervasive changes in architectural education. With advent of what was once called the 'paperless studio' architectural education changed irrevocably. Prior to pursuing the impact of the computer on architectural education it is worth recognizing that changes in the educational practice of

4. The ideas within this paper are developed in a more detailed way in my 'Repositioning Architectural Theory: Towards an Ontology of Techniques', *Architectural Theory Review*, vol. 12, no. 2, 2007, pp. 173-180.

any discipline do not occur in isolation. They are not untouched by political and cultural changes occurring at the same time.

Architectural theory, at the time at which it flourished in the 1980s and 1990s, was part of a general trend within the humanities in which the incorporation of French and German thought transformed disciplines. That transformation was strenuously resisted especially at the institutional level. Sometimes this resistance was successful, as remains the case in philosophy, sometimes it was not. Nonetheless, the self-conception of certain disciplines in the humanities changed dramatically. The impact of what is now called 'post-structuralism' redefined intellectual practice. At the same time as there was an ascendency in theory—a theory that was taken to be inherently progressive—there was a profound disconnect with political developments. Post-structuralism flourished in the period in which Thatcher was the Prime Minister of the United Kingdom and Regan the President of the United States. Their conservative heirs, from Bush to Blair and now in Australia to Rudd, established a lineage of cultural and economic conservatism. The endurance of conservatism remains a continual challenge. The impact of economic rationalism on the structure and practice of the university is overwhelming. Universities as places of critical thought have been muted by continual restructuring and the location of research money outside the university such that a disproportionate amount of time has to be devoted to the attempt to secure research funding. Time that would have been more productively spent doing the research itself.

While it would always have been naïve to imagine that progressive thought could be instrumentalized such that theory on its own could effect social change, nonetheless the move away from theory, a move occurring with an emphatic ubiquity, often in the name of practice, is to concede victory both to the forces of conservatism and to the anti-intellectualism that underpins it. Where the failure of imagination occurs is in the reluctance to concede that there is a relationship to theory that need not be thought within the framework of instrumentality. In the case of the practice of design it is not simply that the move away from theory is part of a more generalized process that could be described as the naturalization of conservatism, a move in which conservatism comes to be equated with the real, it is one that runs the risk of remaining oblivious to the genuine transformations within architectural design.

2.

If there is a genuine point of connection between painting and architecture then it can be located in the presence of techniques. Techniques account not just for the presence of images; they are implicated from the start in the way images are produced. If it is possible to generalize, then what marks techniques today is that the relationship that photography used to have to painting has been replaced by the relation that the digital has to all the forms of image production that preceded it. The history of the image as a consequence demands to be rethought. To reformulate Walter Benjamin's argument, design today takes place in the era of digital reproducibility. Again, it would be too hasty to view the move to the digital as an event that is isolated within the practice of design. Such a development occurs as 'globalization', a term that has replaced both imperialism and internationalism, thereby acquiring, if only initially, a form of neutrality, and is taken as all encompassing. Globalization has also been naturalized such that the only mode of resistance would appear to be forms of atavistic nationalism that have an inherently discordant relation to any conception of modernity. What is opened up thereby is the question concerning what type of resistance might there be to the process of globalization. This is not a question that concerns where architecture is built. Nor is it one that denies that architecture as a practice—as well as architectural practices—work globally.

Globalization has a twofold effect on design. Either it levels design such that what appears is a proliferation of the same, or it reduces specific buildings to aberrant dislocated events whose architectural interest has nothing to do with their actual location. They appear as diamonds in a sea of mud. Countering both these tendencies can only occur effectively with the reintroduction of the region as a domain of architectural thought and practice.

This 'reintroduction' has to be coterminous, however, with the recognition and affirmation of the era of digital reproducibility. Their co-presence announces both the site and the project of architectural theory. The way for the interconnection to be established and thus worked through continually cannot be described as though it only had one form. Digital reproducibility within design opens an importunately new domain of activity. Design now has a relationship to the potentially within software programmes. Design now has modelling abilities—abilities that encompass everything from urban topology to the structural capacity and possibility of space frames—which it had not had hitherto. Theory therefore is given another location. What makes this setting more insistent is that it occurs within and as part of the change of what counts as the design process. And yet, as with all such processes there is the ineliminable risk of formalism. Within the realm of digital reproducibility formalism will have taken on anther guise. If there is a counter to formalism here it necessitates a return to the regional. That return will incorporate the digital however it will allow architecture's implicit urbanism an instructive presence.

What has changed, therefore, with the advent of digital reproducibility is not the need for architectural theory. The contrary is the case. The change is that architectural theory now has a new object. The institutions neglect this new location of intellectual activity at their peril. Neglect will simply allow for a proliferation of formalisms and thus architecture will become a complacent discipline. While able to produce diamonds it will have neglected the mud. While practice may be proffered as a panacea, without the recognition that such a move is simply a game in which professionalism (so-called) will have taken the place of research and as such conservatism will have been rebranded as the real, architecture will have lost its promise. That promise as Adorno once suggested was to think better of people than they think of themselves.[5]

5. For a discussion of the strengths and limits of Adorno's writings on architecture see my 'Allowing Function Complexity: Notes on Adorno's "Functionalism Today"', *AA Files*, no. 41. 2001.

ON THE IMAGE OF DIFFERENT LINES

OPENING IMAGES

As part of any history of lines—a history in which a concern with architecture and the configuration of the urban, come to be pulled through the interplay of geometry and philosophy that predominates in any discussion of the line—the question of appearance can be added. What appears with the line is a question that pertains as much to geometry as it does to the image. Here, however, it is essential to be precise. The question of the architectural image needs to allow for a divide. Though, as with all divisions, there will be important points of overlap, if not imbrication. (And yet, the divide has a necessary insistence one on which it will be possible to insist.)

The divide is, on the one hand, between the image as that which seeks to represent the building—represent it either in the stages of planning or after its having been completed. These representations are as much the photograph as they are the publication of plans and sections. Both form part of the construction of the image. Moreover, both have a complex continuity with the built object. It will be important to return to the question of this complex continuity. On the other hand however, the second element of the divide is a radically different conception of the image. Here, the image is not a representation and yet it is not pure simulacrum. In the place of a simply negative description what has to be argued is that image has become the diagram.[6] What is essential to the diagram is that it is an image, which, while not representational, carries the capacity to generate representations. What will be explored in these notes are the complex consequences and implications of these two different conceptions of the architectural image.

6. For a sustained treatment of the diagram see my *Architectural Philosophy*, Continuum Books, London, 2001.

However, the divide, as has already been intimated, is not strict. Movement across the divide however involves question of constitution and reconstitution. In sense movement involves forms of repetition. Images can be redeployed and repeated. Images have a quality that allows them to be reworked. In the end, it is this capacity of the image to have an afterlife that reveals as much about the ontological status of the architectural image as it does the distinction between representation and diagram. Both moments can themselves be seen as part of a process of allowing for forms of individuation. It would be a mistake therefore to see the difference in question, and the differences enacted by the divide, as lending themselves to a smooth connection, one that would eliminate, in the name of appearance, the real differences in question.

Image as Representation.

The dominant history of the image concerns its relation to an exteriority. What is outside allows for the content of the image to be judged and the quality of the image to be evaluated. The ground of both possibilities is that the image is articulated within a relation between interiority and exteriority. (The exterior oscillates between a transcendental object—Plato, Goethe, etc.—and an empirical designation—e.g. *this* landscape, *that* face etc.) The interiority of the image is its own mode of construction, and the exterior is that which either figures within the image or is involved in any account of how the image is present and what it presents (therefore what it re-presents). The movement does not only go in one direction. There is an important reciprocity here. If the content of a computer screen is taken to be a 2D image that can be realized three dimensionally, or if the image developed by an animation program is already, on the level of appearance, a volume—and therefore can be understood volumetrically—since it involves an 'image' created by the X, Y and Z axes both possibilities can be articulated within a structure of representation. This articulation is possible, as the movement in question has to be understood as occurring between the interior and the exterior. Once this occurs then the image in question is structured by representation. Moreover, it is to be understood in terms of representation.

While the role of the photographic image is a fundamental concern within any account of either the representation of architecture, or architecture's self-representation, what is of central concern is the role of the line. Pursuing the line will allow the problem of the image to be addressed from within a position in which the question of the line's status—the nature of its presence as a specific type of image—is tied to the practice of design.

Operating at an elementary level, the line can be understood as dividing space—it divides it by, in a sense, creating it. Once a line is drawn there are relations of exteriority and interiority. If a line can be extruded such that it becomes a plane then the act of division is significant since what is realized is an extended sense of division. What occurs now with the plane as the extrusion of a line is that a certain potential within a line has been realized. However, because the line is initially defined by a relation between points, the extrusion of the line into the plane, precisely because it can run until infinity, has to be limited by the utilisation of other co-ordinates. Once given, the plane defines a particular space and contains implicit spatial relations. Again, these are relations defined by potential interiors and exteriors. Therefore, while abstract, what is at work here is a division. Two terms dominate even this elementary description. The first is *potential* and the second is *abstract*.

Both these terms indicate that even operating in two dimensions there will always be the possibility to see in the singular a conception of extension. The singular, thus construed, contains a potential. (This indicates something about the nature of singularity, though equally, it also indicates, why potentiality should not be generalized as a descriptive term as though there not different senses of potentiality.) That which has three dimensions can be allowed the potential of a reduction to two dimensions. Moving backward and forward between three dimensions and two dimensions is to realize the way 'potential' operates within this conception of the line. The point at issue is that a two dimensional image can generate a three-dimensional image—whether on the screen or as a projection—and that a three-dimensional image either exterior to the screen or within it can be given a two dimensional expression. Both are possibilities that are inherent in the conception of the line at work within such arguments. The line differs only on the level of quantity between these two possibilities. It should not be thought that potential and abstraction are absent from such a formulation. Rather, the argument is that both potential and abstraction operate within a clearly defined boundary. The line would be defined by the points that initially created it.

Abstraction and potentiality, in this context, are interrelated. What is abstract is that which is prior, priority is held in place by potential. Potential is realized by the abstract line becoming more precise. The movement between dimensions or the movement, more generally the oscillation, between the interior and the exterior—a movement allowing for multidirectionality—indicates in what way a representational conception of the line is articulated within an already constructed discursive field. The interruption of the field involves repeating the line beyond the hold of that field. This repetition 'beyond' may involve forms of sameness on the level of appearance, where this sameness is not repeated, and this despite appearances, is in terms of how the line's effective presence is understood. Again, this is part of the argument against a generalized sense of potential. Once this other possibility is allowed, and that the line can be attributed a productive quality that is not thought in terms of either extrusion or extension, then while it carries potential, that potential has to be understood in an importantly different way. Not only will the line be different and have to be thought differently—even taking appearance into consideration—the presence of potential both in terms of its quality and in how it is to be realized, would necessitate a different theoretical elaboration and as such would have a different set of filiations within the history of philosophy.

THE OTHER IMAGE—THE PRODUCED LINE

Allowing production to become central brings another conception of the line into play. (All lines are produced. The point at issue here is the nature and thus the difference between different senses of production and more significantly the way lines are taken to be productive. This latter element involves, of necessity a consideration of what they produce.) While there is an important additional story in terms of the history of line which moves the line away from a geometry that works by oscillating between two and three dimensions in a relatively unproblematic way, to one that incorporates a repositioning of lines in terms of a spline based geometry, and therefore in terms of complex surfaces, this is not the point at issue here. At this stage what is of significance is the presence of this conception of the line as an image. And thus the use of complex lines to generate images which, while looking as though they are connected to lines that have a readily identifiable directionality, this is a connection that may only take place on the level of appearance. They have to be approached therefore not in terms of the way they appear. Produced lines—produced in the sense of being produced and being productive—complicate the role of appearance.

The appearance of volume, for example, generated by programmes such as Rhino or Maya should not be read automatically volumetrically,—and this has to be case despite the possibility of such an approach. Were this to take place—i.e. the appearance of volume read volumetrically—then the initial diagram would have turned into a series of lines articulated with a structure of representation and thus the initial presentation would have lost its diagrammatic quality. What is at work in the formulation is the necessity of a discontinuity between a diagram and forms of representation. This discontinuity is of fundamental importance. In order to understand some of the issue involved in *the produced line*, a number of the implications of this discontinuity need to be noted. The central issue is in what way working through this discontinuity can open up a concern with the image.

There are several issues that need to be taken up. The first is that what establishes the diagrammatic quality of the diagram is this discontinuity. If the lines were merely different instances given with a general structure of representation, then a smooth connection could be established. The premise however for that relation is that the lines were from the start representational: volume and form were then mere extensions. Once the discontinuity is maintained then the important question that arises concerns the possibility of moving from the diagram to that which sustains representation. The question concerns the move from diagram to architectural form. The strategic issue is that form generation concerns that which will interrupt the discontinuity in order to release the representational potential in the diagram.

Before pursuing this point there is a related point of fundamental importance that needs to be noted. It concerns the reverse procedure. In this instance what were initially straightforwardly representational lines would be read diagrammatically. Once read in this way—and this is the possibility alluded to earlier in regards to constituting and reconstituting lines beyond shifts understood quantitatively by allowing repetitions to introduce real differences—then the question of how to move to representation and therefore how to generate real architectural form becomes a matter of negotiating the discontinuity that would have been (re-) established by reworking the representation as a diagram. What is central once again is the discontinuity. Indeed, what cannot be avoided is the need to maintain the discontinuity by having to work through. One of the consequences of the inevitability of this movement through the discontinuity is that form is the consequence of the line's potential and as such could never be the direct iteration of the original diagram's appearance. Once a set-up of this nature can be maintained then what has to be worked with is the realization that there is not a necessary formal implication inherent in a given diagram. Hence the move from diagram to form cannot be a simple extension, let alone a formal repetition.

If what is of fundamental importance in both instances—the first being the move from diagram to representation and the second the reworking of an original representational model as a diagram—is that a discontinuity is established, then the question is always going to be the interruption of that discontinuity. Interruption will be simultaneous with form generation. A way of understanding the complexity of this situation is by beginning with the position that the diagram can allow for at least two different forms of research. The first can be linked to the production of programmatic diagrams and the second to diagrams investigating volume. The same project therefore generates different sets of diagrammatic analyses. Each set brings with it the general problem of the production of form. (Lines have to be productive.) Whether one set of diagrams is used to interrupt another is not, in this instance, the point. What is of real significance is the possibility of different domains of diagrammatic research. The initial diagrams identify the founding site of research. However, while founding it generates another. The second occurs from the necessity of having to work through the discontinuity. However, this will involve an important shift in how research is undertaken. Fundamental to what is meant by 'working through' is freeing the diagrammatic from any necessary entailment in regard to form. What this means is that the locus of the discontinuity becomes the site of architectural experimentation.

Without the discontinuity and therefore working with the assumption that the question of form—if only on the level of appearance—had already been resolved, then all experimentation would be is the confirming of what is already known. Once the discontinuity is allowed to hold sway then rather than experimentation being constrained by prediction and formal expectation, it becomes inextricably tied to invention. Precisely because inventions need not be successful, and more significantly since there will be many ways of allowing for the release of a potential within an initial diagram, what also emerges is that the discontinuity—its being worked through—is the initial site of judgement.

What occurs therefore with the produced line understood as the diagram, is a fundamentally different sense of the image. While architecture as a design practice and as an object of historical and theoretical study works with, and through, images, what has to be argued is that there are fundamentally different senses of image at work in, and within, each instance. Allowing for a discontinuity to define the way of moving between the various images of architecture, is to allow for the particularity of the different domains of practice. In every instance difference will involve the centrality of techniques since the move from image to image—diagram to representation, for example,—involves working through sites of discontinuity. The impossibility of a purely formal or theoretical extension—impossible if the discontinuity is to endure as the site engendering work—means that the different ways through are bound up with the techniques that allow them to be realized. Judgement therefore has to take the nature of the experimentation, its formal resolution and the techniques enabling it to occur as its object.

Finally, what emerges from these working notes is that the capacity for images to be positioned and repositioned; for lines to allow for discontinuity; for a discontinuity to be the ground of form, means that the history of lines has to allow for more than the inclusion of lines into discursive fields. Images and lines—the image of lines—will have had a founding plurality that allows them to be reworked and repositioned. The capacity for the line eventually to fold and yet for the fold to be held back from any immediate move to form, means that form and particularity are finite moments within a field of a potential infinite. In sum, finitude is both the result of the interruption and of what interrupts. The question will always be how, in any one instance, is finitude to figure. What will its appearance be?

VISUAL MEMORY
Whiteread and Eisenman

Haunting every public act of memory—be it the action of architecture or sculpture—is the threat of a forgetting occasioned by the act having vanished. Vanishing, of course, need not be literal. Once the memorial has been absorbed or assimilated, then what is intended to have been recalled will remain on the edge of being forgotten. Mere physical presence cannot stem the possible interplay of vanishing and forgetting. There is, however, a counter move. It begins with the recognition that absorption is as much an aesthetic concern as it is an urban one. Another aesthetic dimension needs to be brought into play. If the memorial is to be linked to remembering then it must refuse decorum. Refusing by not allowing the memorial's surrounds to order either its position or its appearance. The memorial therefore needs a strong sense of disorder. Disorder becomes an activity. The work—the act of memory—needs to dis-order. As though through acts of dis-ordering, acts that are inherently creative and not simply destructive, dis-order will have become a verb, whose imperative form—*dis-order*—will aid in orchestrating the creation of public acts of memory. Equally, it must guide the interpretation of such acts.

What is demanded therefore—demanded by the necessity to resist the moment in which vanishing and forgetting coalesce in the memorial's final assimilation—are strategies that allow a continual resistance to order. Opening up as a result, a creative approach that works within what could be described as logic of disordering. Such logic is neither an anti-aesthetic, nor equally does it signal the end of a concern with design. If fact, in both instances, the opposite is the case. Dis-order is not nihilism, it is the recognition that public acts of memory bring with them differing conceptions of historical time, differing practices of design and alternative conceptions of particularity. Public acts of memory are only ever specific. What is recalled—memorialized and therefore retained through a work of memory articulated within public space by differing design strategies—will always have its own unique history. While forming part of a general history, the public memorial must address not just the particularity of a given event, or a given set of circumstances; the nature of the particular—and therefore how that particular instance is understood and interpreted—will have determining effect on the appearance of the final design. (As though there could be only one design proper to each act of public memory.) It will not structure the design in advance. Rather, it will construct the parameters within which the design occurs. To the extent that disordering is maintained particularity becomes the site of complex and unpredictable design practice. Memory opens up within design as the realization of potentiality.

What then is a logic of disordering? Prior to answering this question the alternative needs to be noted. It would involve maintaining public order. Such a move would be unproblematic if public order were not itself the site of contestation. In the Australian context for example, reconciliation is a site—a public site—of political conflict. A contestation whose differing forms of resolution will give rise to different design considerations. In other words, the order of public space is an already determined one. An order resulting from the way a certain political play of forces is configured at a given moment. Interrupting that order is to disorder. Disordering however will only ever be effective if the design strategy—strategy in the broadest sense of the term—has a holding effect within the public realm. To be beheld by a memorial is to respond. In the place of simple distraction, intervention within, and as part of, the public realms must have an affective quality. The creation of affect holds out against the threat of forgetting.

Affect however is not mere sensation. Within the public realm a memorial is effective to the extent that it is inextricably bound up with particularity. Two instances will indicate how such a possibility may be realized. Both concern Holocaust memorials. That both have a determined content is precisely what allows them to have an exemplary force. Generality is without utility. Since the project of the public memorial does not have only one form, addressing specific instances can be instructive.

Peter Eisenman's Memorial to the Murdered Jews of Europe is situated in Berlin. It was officially opened in May 2008. While always contestable, the need for such memorials continues. Eisenman's memorial consists of a series of pillars emerging from the ground. The area of more than 2 hectares is an undulating surface from which the pillars arise. The site contains over 3500 pillars varying in size from .5m and 2.5m. The distance between them is such than no matter how the body is positioned there is always a sense of a refusal of place. The logic of disordering works by providing a sense of location that dislocates. While the site will contain educational material, the Memorial's power—power as affect—occurs through a sense of productive abstraction. The abstraction of the pillars is effective. The pillars recall gravestones and yet they are not just gravestones. What they stand for is a sense of loss and therefore they insist as forms of remembrance. However, it is their abstract quality, in other words their refusal to provide an image, which determines their power. How and what they represent remains open. Part of that openness is a questioning of the very possibility of there being an appropriate image. Once posed, the question of the appropriate image defines the memorial's operative quality. That quality is not there as a meaning to be attached to matter. It is a consequence of the way matter works in and through scale. Over the site there are thousands of pillars. Affect here is the result of materiality and scale.

While radically different, Rachel Whiteread's memorial in Judenplatz in Vienna, built almost ten years ago, uses scale to achieve its effect. In appearance the cast presence of a book lined room has moved from the interior to the exterior. Moving the interior to the exterior gives the work an enigmatic quality. While debatable, the centrality given to the book defines—in a number of different senses—the obvious connection between Judaism and the book. The power of the project does not lie in its content as though affect had a direct relation to meaning. Affect in this instance can only be accounted for properly by reference to scale and materiality. In terms of both building material and colour the memorial's location in the square becomes the identification of a form of residence—the object is as much a house as it is a form of box—detached from the buildings themselves and yet forming part of the square. The nature of belonging is complicated by the memorial's 'fact' of belonging and yet its clear sense of not belonging. What allows this meditation on belonging to continue is the interplay of scale and matter. The size of this house made of books, in relation to the rest of Judenplatz, is such that it works to dis-order the order demanded by both the geometry, materiality and scale of the square itself.

Visual memory is possible to the extent that matter retains an insistence quality. Insistence is not spectacle. The spectacle can always occasion its own forgetting. Insistence necessitates that particularity is maintained within the pervasive hold of dis-order. The presence of dis-order demands a critical defence that will always assume that public opinion has the same quality as public order; i.e. both are sites of conflict and disputation. Real visual memory demands nothing less.

PERFORMING, EFFECTING SURFACES

> *Art in its highest exaltation hates exegesis; it therefore immediately shuns the emphasis on meaning.*
>
> Gottfried Semper

As lines knot intensities emerge that begin to take on the possibility of form. These lines are as much the marks of movement as they are the conveyors of information. To be precise, of course, the lines neither mark nor convey—they *are* movement and information. Understanding this shift—a shift in which a structure of representation is displaced by another conception of the line—forms an integral part of what is necessary to the work of Dagmar Richter. Once lines are given the extension they need such that they come to define a field of activity, then rather than a line which can do no more than mark the distance between two points, they acquire the quality of a surface.

Richter's work forms a fundamental part of a specific trajectory within contemporary architectural practice. As opposed to the production of computer generated surfaces that are then given volumetric expression, there is the use of what will be described as the *surface effect*—what Richter refers to as 'performing surfaces'.[7] As is made clear in the texts accompanying the project descriptions, the lineage of this approach runs from at least Semper, through Loos, up to the present. But, while having certain accuracy, such a formulation would misconstrue the history involved and thus fail to grasp the significance of this work. Rather than the passage of time leading to the current situation, something else is at stake. With the development of computer software that allows

7. This text first appeared as the introduction to a volume presenting Richter's recent work in which she develops the idea of the 'performing surfaces.' See Dagmar Richer, *Armed Surfaces*, Black Dog Press, London, 2003.

for the construction of surfaces that work to distribute elements of architecture as much as programme and programmable space, there is a different exigency. What these developments demand is a recasting of the history, such that a history of the surface can be written from the position of the present.

Semper's insistence on a distinction between the wall as that which brings about spatial enclosure and the wall as load bearing redefines the wall's presence. Once the wall's presence is no longer reducible to the literal wall, it attains a freedom such that it is possible to talk of 'the wall effect'.[8] And once this position is connected to his writings on textiles and materials, what emerges is an undertaking that links the project of architecture and its realization to the work of materials.[9] What is important, however, is that those materials have the capacity to define the particularity of a given project by positioning the surface as distributing programme. To the extent that the wall effect can be realized by the work of the surface, it is also possible that the surface can distribute other foundational architectural elements. There is no *a priori* reason, for example, to think that furniture cannot be an effect of the surface. Once the surface becomes productive, and this is the potential that is there in Semper, though equally in Loos for whom the intersection of the 'Raumplan' and cladding opens up the work of the surface effect, another history of architecture becomes possible.[10]

Architects, of whom Richter is one, who begin with the surface—the surface as productive and thus defined in terms of becoming—can move between an interest in the surface, the computer generated surface as a diagram, and the way materials can combine to create literal surfaces that effect. The surface involves therefore two dimensions, the surface as diagram and the surface as material enactment. They combine in particular ways in given projects.

The presence of the surface as a diagram allows for specific modes of investigation. In DomestiCity the rigid distinction between public and private, where the presence of walls defines the

8. I have taken up this question in my 'Notes on the Surfacing of Walls. Semper, Kiesler, NOX', In *Machining Architecture*, Thames and Hudson, London, 2004.

9. See my 'Plans to Matter: Towards a History of Material Possibility', in Katie Lloyd-Thomas (ed.) *Material Matters*, Routledge.

10. I have addressed the question of a history of the surface—albeit a history written from the position of the present in my—'The Surface Effect: Borromini, Semper, Loos', *Journal of Architecture*, vol. 11, no. 1, 2006, pp. 1-36.

limits of the possible, is overcome by acts of architectural extension. By distributing functions and thus reprogramming spaces as at once private and public, the dispersed subject has a home. While the house retains its particularity, the spread of personal activities through apparently 'public' space and the inscription of the activities of the complex subjectivity of modernity into the house is enacted through the drawing of lines of dispersal through and across urban fields. At this level there is generality and yet it is precisely because there is an abstract form of the general that there can be particularization. If this is prototyping then it has taken a unique form. Rather than the model of the trainer or the automobile, here there is actual singularity. Prototyping has to break with a conception of production that is delimited by the reiteration, no matter how intricate, of Sameness. The real strength of this project lies, in part, in Richter's insistence on the co-presence of the 'unique'—it is after all *my* house—and the recognition that permanence has become impermanence. The latter need not be literal. There is no need for what she calls the 'nomadic generation' to be without any sense of place. Rather the relationship between the domestic and the urban—beautifully captured in the term *DomestiCity*—is redefined by *performing surfaces* that weave together what were initially understood as mutually exclusive terms. These weaves create diagrams. The move to form—the diagram's architectural resolution—is not to construe the diagram volumetrically. Performing surfaces are as much an analysis as suggestive of a resolution that will necessitate realizing abstraction's inherent potential.

The Waterford Crystal project once again deploys the interplay of surface and diagram. In this instance instead of starting with a surface that carried information in any straightforward sense, the material surface of crystals became the point of departure. There are two elements of this approach that need to be noted, both attest to the power of Richter's work. The first concerns what will be described as the necessity for interruption and the second, architectural experimentation. Experimentation, as will be suggested, deploys the relationship between the abstract and the particular. However, it should be noted that it is not the relationship between the universal and the particular, since such a mode of thinking is antithetical to the work of diagrams and surfaces that characterise Richter's recent projects.

One of the problems inherent in constructing surfaces through the use of animation software is defining the point at which the animation should be brought to an end. The risk of formalism lies in the absence of a constraint that is external to the logic of the animation itself. While one way of interrupting such a procedure can occur by the use of a programmatic diagram that intersects the volumetric one, Richter intersects the immateriality of the computer generated surface via an engagement with physical surfaces and their inherent constraints. Hair and crystals provided sites of investigation in order to identify properties that would allow for points of intersection between the material and the immaterial to be noted. While the use of crystals bears an important connection to the history of Waterford, the property of the crystals themselves was just as indispensable in allowing for the creation of productive surfaces.

Once constraints can be established, then instead of this resulting in finished products, it needs to be understood as creating sites in which both models and ideas can be tested. The re-presentation of Waterford as a complex object of mirrored surfaces results from the interplay of the immaterial and the material. Instead of there having been the rush to finality—as though either a simple analysis or an elementary animation are generative of built form—Waterford re-emerged as a diagram that was able to incorporate architectural interventions. The surface did not function as an image guiding the project. Richter deployed different senses of the surface to recreate, for architecture, Waterford as a diagram. This level of abstraction was the condition allowing for a specific intervention. Once again, the prototype attains particularity and thus can address the concerns of a given town or region only on the precondition of abstraction.

A similar strategy can also be found in the Dom-in(f)o House. Prior to noting—albeit briefly—the particularity of that research project, it is essential to reiterate the significance of this undertaking. As has already been intimated, contemporary research in architecture can be driven by form creation to the point where it circles back upon itself to meet work occurring under the rubric of 'form follows function'. In both instances the dominance of form creation make programmatic concerns devoid of specificity. At no point could these concerns be allowed to have any impact on form creation.

Richter's move is from Le Corbusier's Domino House, which she views as restricting architectural intervention to no more than the cladding or aestheticizing of an 'engineered architecture', to the Dom-in(f)o House in which the surface is present as structure.

While this is a move that is occasioned by initially rendering the skeleton through the application of animation software, the smooth relations that are then constructed cannot be viewed as ends in themselves. Indeed, the contrary is the case. The transformation means that the House is now a site in which different modalities of habitation—polis dwelling—can be tested. While the tests are formal in nature, each formal transformation is intended to open up for evaluation other possibilities for housing and living. Here, Richter emerges as an architect of the political, rather than as a merely political architect.

Part of what is demonstrated here is the limitation of the apparent freedom of the Domino frame. Only the transformations resulting from the smoothing of the elements allows it to be 'bombarded with contemporary performance criteria'. As such, new domestic and social conditions can be investigated from within the activity of design itself.

Dagmar Richter's work opens up a way beyond the formalism in which the appearance of the architecture of animation software is simply the realization of the diagram and thus is the effacing of the diagrammatic. Equally, it allows for programme to be central to production. It is not surprising that she always connects—perhaps inter-articulates—experimentations with surfaces and political, cultural and theoretical concerns. Surfaces perform, when they allow. Surfaces effect, when they realize. Allowing and realizing are modes of freedom that have to be marked by actuality. They are not the idealized freedoms that the oscillation between utopianism and formalism enacts. Rather, they involve the creation of openings that create different possibilities by giving them a place. How they are then lived with, is the question that makes the future, even if unpredictable, a concern of the present.

A SECULAR TEMENOS

Notes on the addition to the Shrine of Remembrance

With ARM's addition to the Shrine of Remembrance in Melbourne and Rush/Wright's Masterplan for the Shrine Reserve—an 11 ha site incorporating the actual Shrine—two architectural concerns can be said to predominate. The first involves the insertion of program into a pre-existing building, one that already has both iconic and programmatic importance within Melbourne. The second is allowing for a differentiation of the Shrine Reserve within the Domain Parklands. The defining factor of this second concern is that the differentiation must occur as an effect of the landscape rather than the insertion of simple boundaries. These concerns overlap at a number of important points. Detailing these concerns becomes the articulation, and evaluation, of architectural resolutions to what could always be described as problems having greater generality.

What characterizes War Memorials in general in both Australia and New Zealand is that they commemorate service in the Forces rather than simply honouring those who died. Memorials, in this context therefore, have a different sense of occasion. While functioning as important locations of memorialization, they are also imbued with the need to house a more complex program. The necessity to allow both for the memory of the dead and the continuity of recognition for those who served, and who continue to serve, creates therefore a different project. Moreover, the highly contested nature of war, the impossibility of simple glorification and yet the necessity for forms acknowledgment, introduces another set of constraints.

This is the context in which it is essential to locate ARM's Shrine of Remembrance project. Responding to the need to create sites for administration, display and educational activity, the problems were always going to be the visual quality of the addition and the effect on the already present structure. The intrusion of most of the program beneath the existing structure has a number of important consequences. The first is that the visual registration of the addition is given by the geometry of the exterior walls that flank either side of the front. Their symmetry comes not from the plan but their relation to the geometry of the original shrine. The use of entasis in the original Hudson & Wardrop building—completed in 1933 as the result of a public subscription—means that the symmetry of the original is created by angles of projection as much as a simple relation between the horizontal and the vertical. The layering of the elements comprising the new exterior wall—producing a faceted wall—has to be understood as a contemporary architectural response to the original form. The question is, of course, what makes it contemporary? Part of the answer is to be found in the way that contemporary design processes and materials do not mime the original but to pick up both its organizing geometry and then to reiterate the work of a geometry that has both an immediate effect and a projected one. The question of symmetry therefore is especially interesting in this context. Looking at the overall plan, the Entry Courtyard and the Garden Court are symmetrical in terms of location. The symmetry of the elevation however is given by the geometry of the initial building. What this means is that there is no need to define the symmetry of these elements internally—e.g. by the use of circular walls. The consequence of this rethinking of their position is that both the Entry Courtyard and the Garden Court can take on an individual quality while the overall order of the addition and its relation to the existing building is maintained.

The addition will mean that entry to the shine will take place through the added courtyard. Entry will occur through a display area in which all the medals marking military activity will be mounted on a wall running almost the entire length of the addition. Set into the ground beneath the wall is a display of poppies. (Cunningham Martyn Design created this aspect of the interior design.) While for the most part relatively straightforward in terms of its operation, there are two programmatic elements of the addition that demand further consideration; in the first place the courtyard and the garden, and in the second the way the addition has opened up the Shrine by establishing a new connection to the

Crypt. What is significant about the connection is that it opens up the Shrine in a way that the original plan did not envisage but yet does not preclude. Movement from the arcade to the Crypt takes place through an area in which the original columns are revealed. The height of the roof taken in conjunction with the columns creates a sanctuary; one imbued with a certain sanctity coming as much from its positioning in relation to the Crypt as the way the light of the Crypt illuminates it. The addition releases this potential. The newly created volume is programmed by its location between the addition and the Crypt. Here is an instance where it could be said that it is the architecture that does the work.

The Entry Courtyard, not only provides a new visual relationship with the Shrine, a state of affairs that is repeated in its own way in the Garden Court, the faceted walls deals with the question of monumentality in original ways. While the wall's organizational geometry works to disclose a space that is more than a simple forecourt, other elements are of real significance. Their projected colour, perhaps recalling the colour of the original edition of Bean's *History of The First World War*, raises interesting questions. Not only does it allow for the problem of colour in architecture to be posed, the question of the colour appropriate to the process of memorialization is raised and, in part, resolved. The reason why it is possible to suggest that there is a partial resolution has to do with the inherently secular nature of the site. What is significant about the Shrine is that rather than being religious in character is has to do with the relations between community and memory. Colour is deployed in order to give this relation—a relation eschewing the directly religious—a more contemporary presentation. ARM's use of colour, as with the use of hand writing almost as a contemporary plaque—the words 'lest we forget' are written across the walls—can be understood as their attempt to give architectural resolutions to these specific issues of memorialization. The specific colour in not having a determined point of reference creates a site whose meaning is not given in advance. ARM's refusal of the symbol marks an important departure.

The Garden Court has allowed the landscape architects Rush/Wright a place to work within ARM's overall project. The Garden takes up the theme of the creation of a setting that involves reverence and a sense of sobriety while articulating both within an architectural language that is inherently secular in nature. The garden is designed to pick up the organizational lead given by the walls. The introduction of a circulation path, yielding places of repose, establishes a place of reflection. The presence of an olive tree in the middle works to recall the interplay of war and peace while resisting any immediate form of glorification. The sobriety is reinforced by the view of the Shrine afforded by the garden. The visual effect heightens the function of the garden as a site of reflection.

The addition to the Shrine occurs in the context of a new Masterplan by Rush/Wright for the Shrine Reserve. The plan envisages the creation of an area for the Shrine that will have a distinct location in the overall reserve. Boundaries will be established by a reworking of the contours, a tree removal and planting plan and the construction of a new grassland policy. If there is a guiding motif for the plan it has to do with the problem of continuity and renewal as raised by this site. Of the many elements that could be taken from Hudson & Wardrop's commitment to a form of Classicism is the possibility of reusing the relationship between Temple and site that had such an important effect on Greek architecture. As archaeological evidence bears out the Temple can never be divorced from the site. What exists is a temenos. (This is the term that Rush/Wright also use in the documentation.) If this is the point of departure, then the question is how is this relationship between temple and site to be understood now? What is a modern temenos? While part of the answer to that question involves shifts in the landscape, it is only be recognizing that the landscaping is an architectural response to the creation of a site that while having aspects of the sacred is not counter posed to the profane. Such opposition is simply unacceptable to any modern sensibility. And yet, if the modern cannot allow for any sense of sanctuary, then the possibility of a real site of memory—architectural acts of memorialization—would have become impossible. The resolution here in terms of landscaping is to address the question of the differentiation of the Shrine reserve and the internal operation of that reserve in terms of access and movement. In general the relationship between contours and movement will work to identify the site. What will define the area as a modern temenos is that the movement into the site will involve crossing a threshold—one created as an effect of the landscaping and hence one that has to be understood as architectural. As a result there will be a shift in the quality of public space. The modern temenos depends both on the public nature of architecture—and thus the public as both modern and secular—and yet for a complex sense of the public and thus public space to emerge as a consequence.

There is therefore a real affinity between the two projects. It is not just that they are intended to work together, they can both be understood as architectural responses to the question of how today does it become possible to deal with the reality of war and service without falling into the trap created by 'God and Country'.

RESISTING THE DESIGN OF EMPIRE
Notes on Bruce Mau's Massive Change

Design brings with it a series of pretensions. While within design there may be an implicit politics, perhaps the greatest pretension that design can have is the suggestion that it can supplant the political. And yet, it is not difficult to understand how such an eventuality might emerge, even if only as a possibility within thought. One of the frustrating though nonetheless insistent aspects of contemporary political life is not just the inability to see an oppositional politics articulated within the divisions constructing the political, in the Australian context between the Labor and Liberal parties, but the absence of a clearly identified locus for the expression of any oppositional position at all. There are a number of important consequences of such a description of the political. One is to continue to work through the operation of a counter culture. Activities that are parasitic upon both pre-existing institutions and infrastructures but which resist—or attempt to resist—complete incorporation. Maintaining counter sites of cultural, intellectual and political activity does not involve the naivety of utopianism. It demands strategies of insertion and activity, which, by resisting the immediate demands of instrumentality, can be more adequately described as resulting in a politics of the event. Politics in which the event has an inherent plurality. As a result of this plurality such a positioning works within both partiality and incompleteness. What is at stake is the development of a politics of productive resistance. A politics that assumes the necessity of the event's plurality.

Another response, antithetical to the one outlined above and in which it is possible to locate the work of Bruce Mau, involves the acceptance of the formulations and determination of existing orders. Within it political agency cannot be defined in terms of a locus of activity delimited by the event. Rather it occurs by a muting of the political as a result of the political having been absorbed within the practice of design. The political as a site of conflict would have been effaced within the project possibility of endless forms of relationality. The relations in question would only ever be conjunctive. Having to negotiate the inevitability of disjunction is precisely the possibility against which design would have been marshalled.

These opening reflections, ones which will always need to be spelled out in much greater detail, provide the locus for another assessment of the project of Bruce Mau's recent book *Massive Change* and the body from which it arose The Institute Without Boundaries.[11]

Within the book and superimposed on a photo of the container port at Hong Kong—a photograph it should be added that demands both in terms of its aesthetic quality and the conception of density it displays a different analysis—are the words 'We will seamlessly integrate all supply and demand around the world'. Slogans of this nature are interposed with analysis and interviews with members of the Institute. What characterizes them is what could be described as generalized strategies of smoothing. What is wanted is not just a more efficient version of what is; rather, it is to design the avoidance of the catastrophic. (This will occur because 'We will build a global mind'.) Efficiency would necessitate ironing out the wrinkles and with their elimination the creation of flows and the seamless. Attributing centrality to movement would no longer necessitate local agreement. Agreement would have been generalized. This can only be achieved—or at least this is the contention of the Institute—through the practice of design. It is as though the political understood as involving conflicts and the disequilibrium of power will have been effaced in the name of design. However, the question that needs to be asked must concern the implicit politics of such a strategy.

Flows of capital necessitate the absence of boundaries. And yet, such a desire is complicated, for example, by the refusal by certain nation states to accept agreements regulating the world environment. That refusal is, of course, the reimposition of boundaries. Both Australia's and America's initial refusal of the Kyoto Accord is a clear instance of this reimposition. The case for the

11. Bruce Mau, *Massive Change*, Phaidon, London, 2004.

rejection of this specific agreement is that it will interfere with the more general one concerning the flow of capital. Any subsequent adoption would always have to involve giving priority to the complex flows of capital rather than to any measure stemming them. However, it is not as though there is simply the movement of money and resources that mark the operation of the world economy. There is an inherent operation of power within it. Resisting he operative presence of power—power in its inevitable multiplicity—cannot just be done in the name of the boundless, even if it is given within an idealized conception of boundless universality. The proposition that design, working on the level of a general economy, can overcome the aporias of contemporary political and economic life is not flawed because it is naive. It may be. The flaw lies in the failure to understand the way in which the strategies of smoothing are already integrated into the operation of the world economy. An economy structured by a hierarchy of concerns. As such Mau's project and the philosophical thought underpinning it give rise to design's adoption and incorporation of the logic of capital

If countering its operation is a priority, then not only will this necessitate rethinking the nature of resistance, it will also involve giving related consideration to terms such as *place, region* and the *cosmopolitan*. Rather than a politics of total design, what becomes essential is the articulation of design within a regionalized politicization of geography. A strategy whose operative dimension will eschew the national and the vernacular in the name of diversity and density within the local. The latter gives a priority to resistance. Such a prioritization is compatible with a politics of the plural event. Precisely because change—massive or not—will not be instituted other than within boundaries, the practice of design and politics is to reimagine the productive intersection of the boundless and the boundary. Perhaps this will necessitate introducing catastrophic wrinkles rather than smoothing them out in the name of a version of efficiency. After all, for whom is the seamless a necessity?

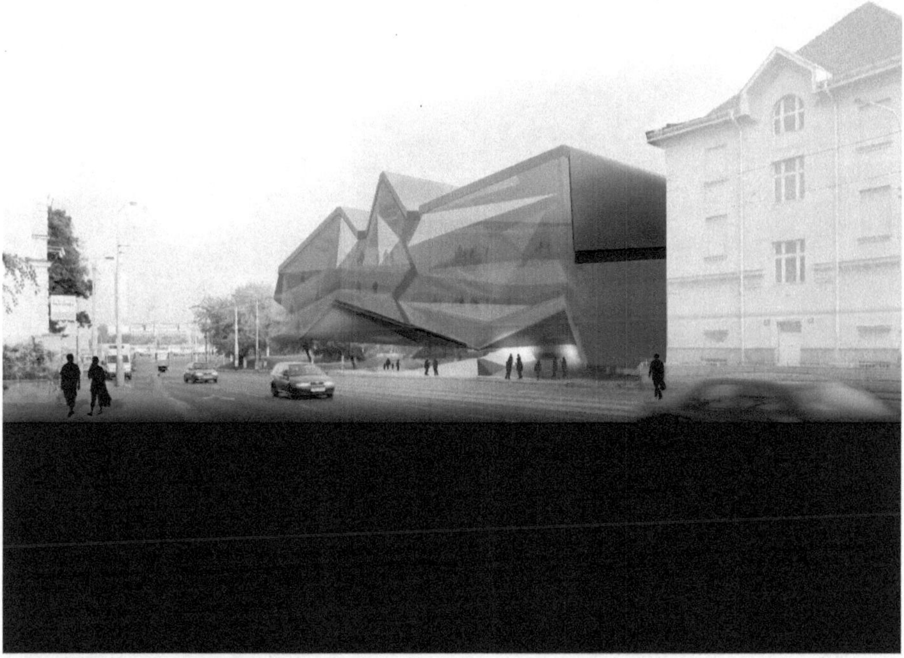

01. Terroir, *Prague Library competition entry*, exterior, 2007.

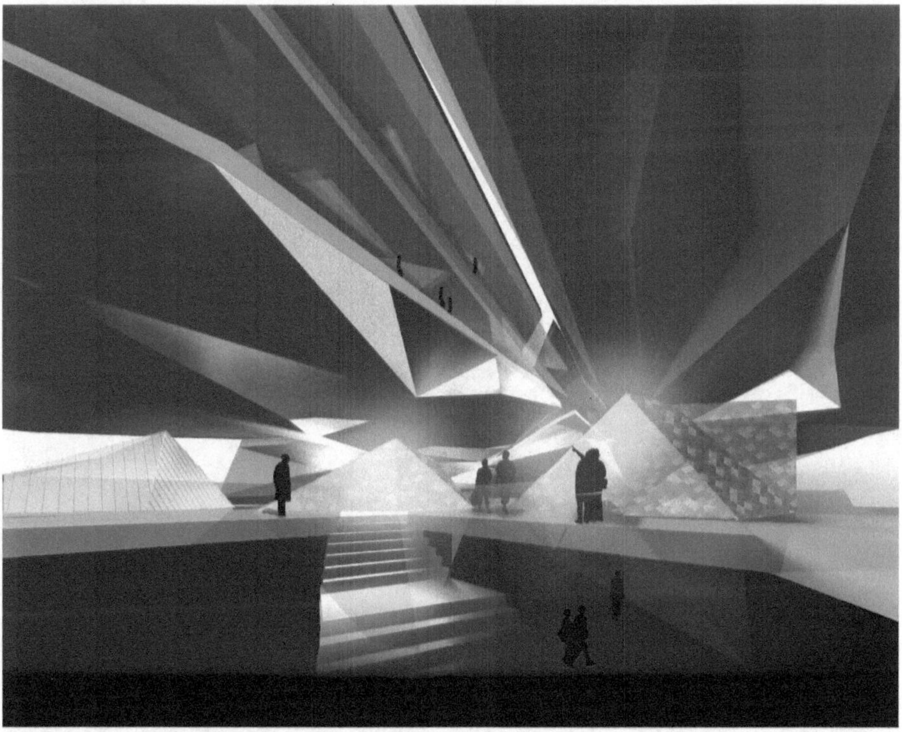

02. Terroir, *Prague Library competition entry*, interior, 2007.

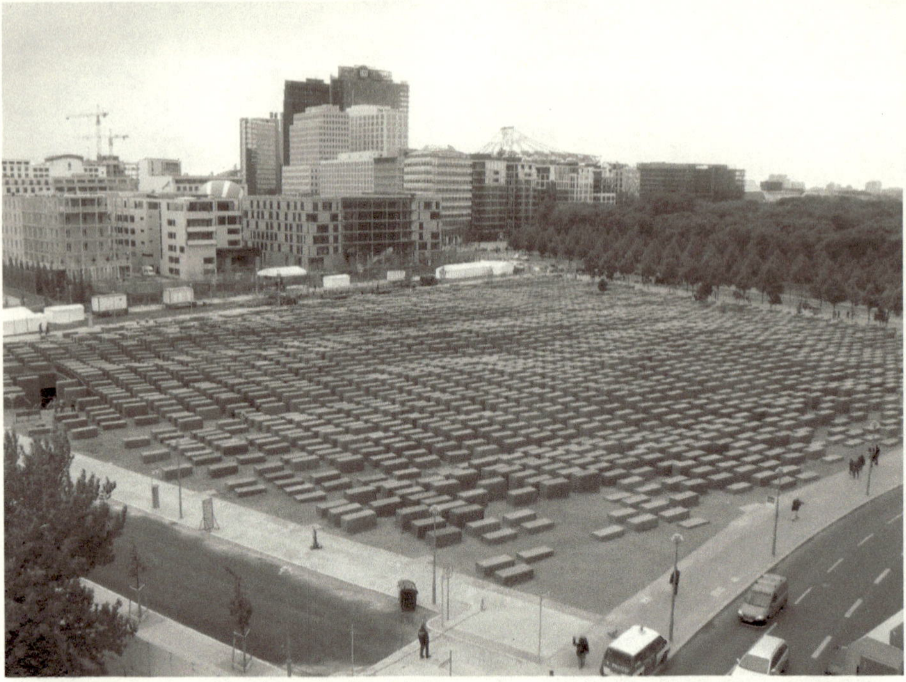

03. Peter Eisenman, *Memorial to the Murdered Jews of Europe*, 2004.

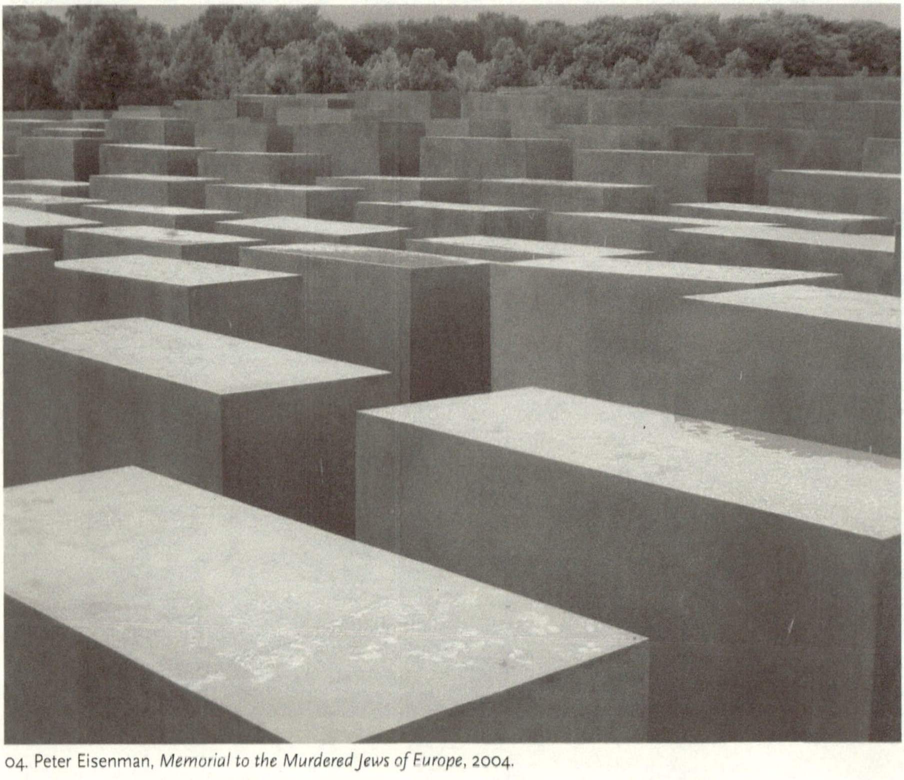

04. Peter Eisenman, *Memorial to the Murdered Jews of Europe*, 2004.

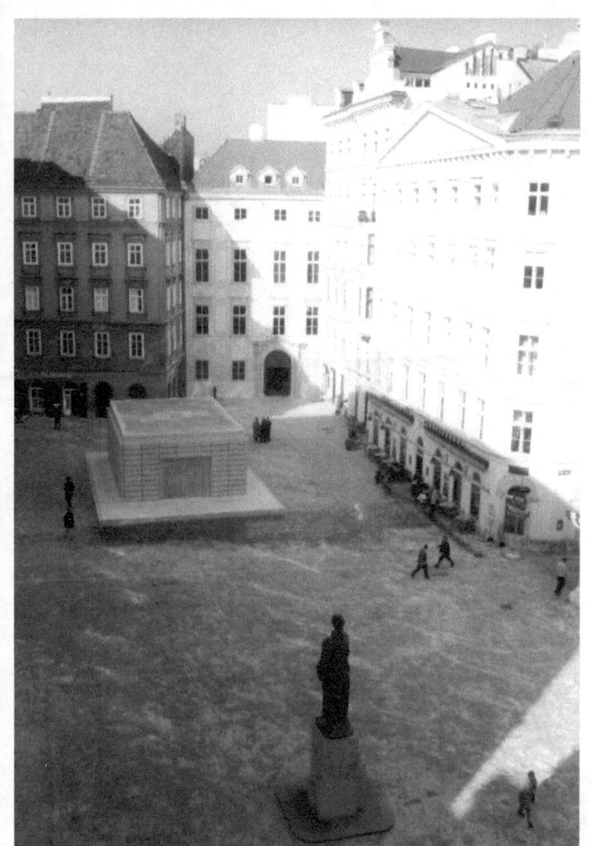

05. Rachel Whiteread, *Judenplatz Holocaust Memorial*, 2000.

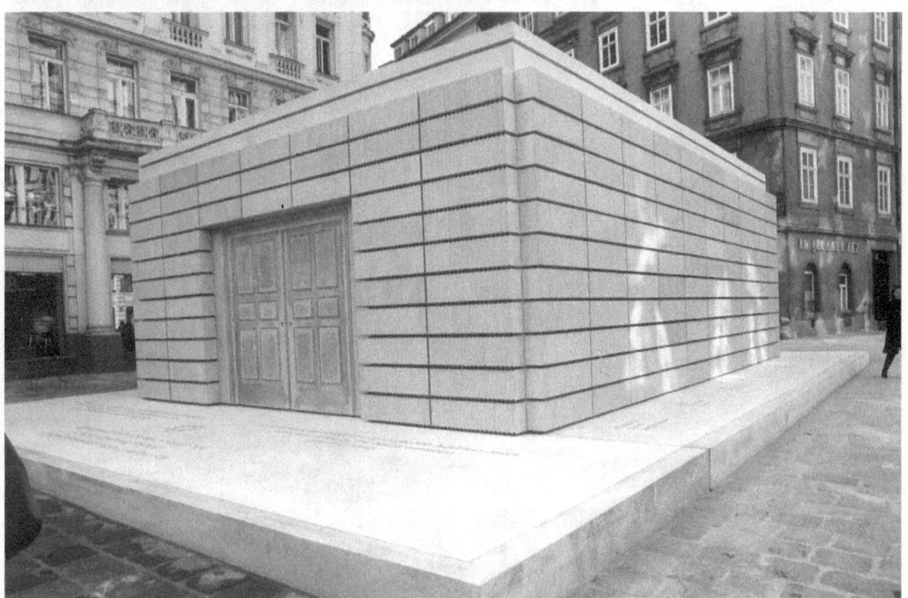

06. Rachel Whiteread, *Judenplatz Holocaust Memorial*, 2000.

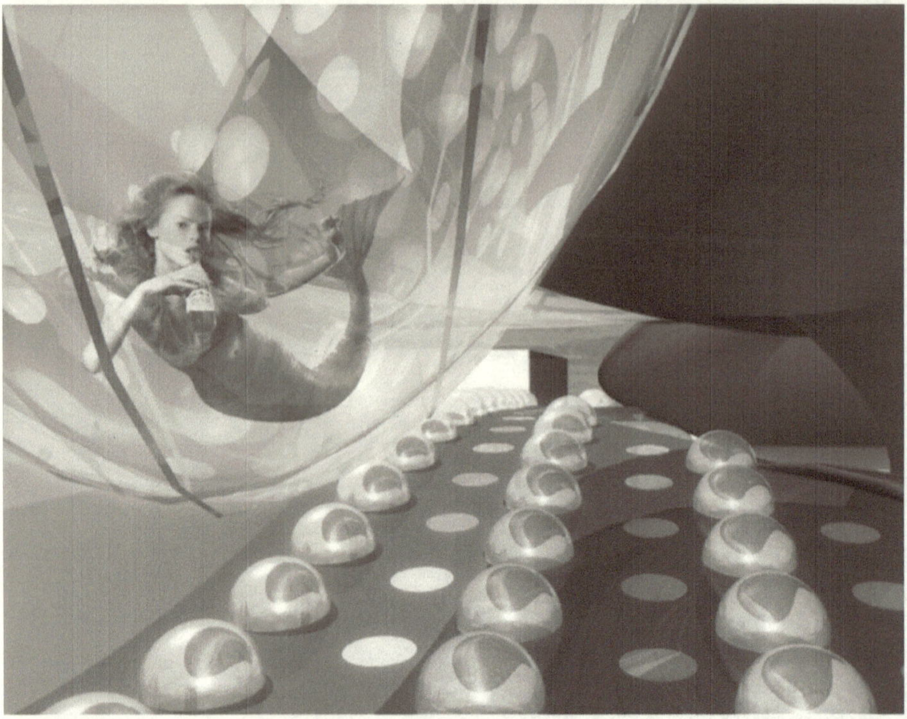

07. Dagmar Richter, *The Domesti-City Project (Rendering of interior).*

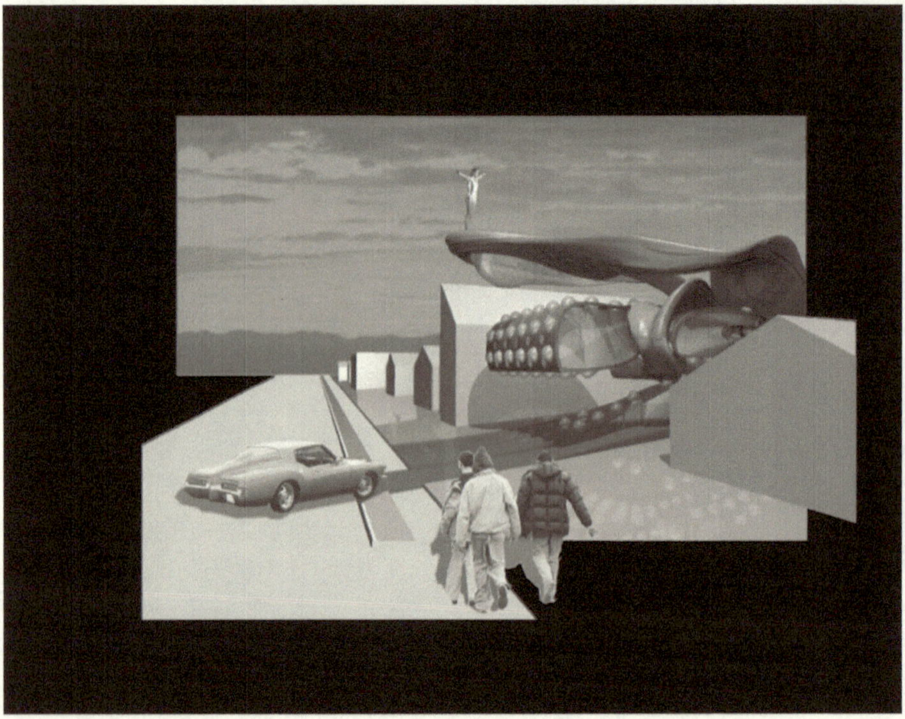

08. Dagmar Richter, *The Domesti-City Project (Rendering of non-building exterior from street).*

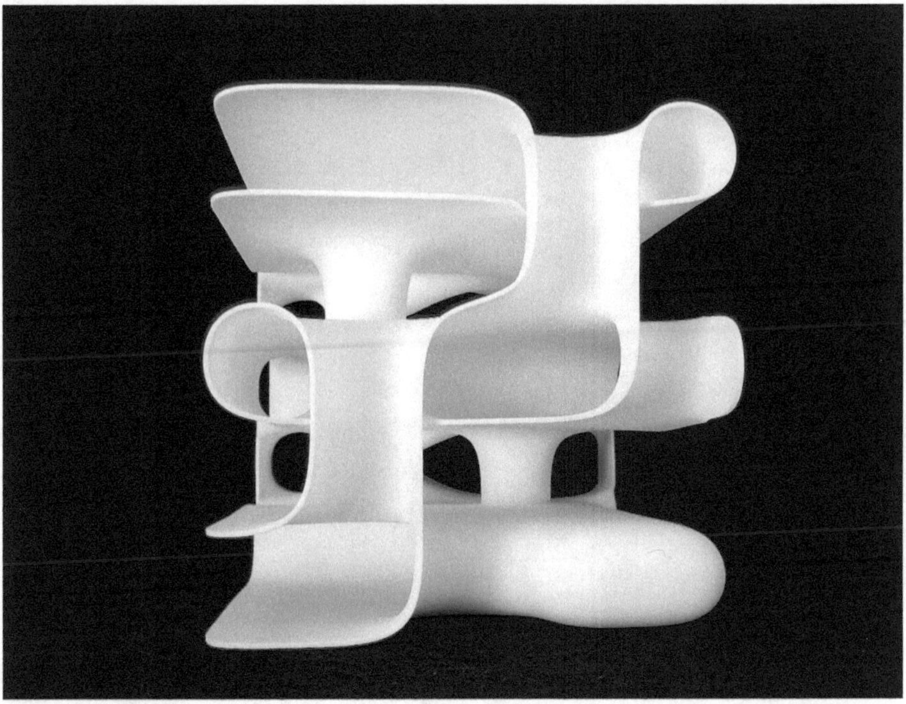

09. Dagmar Richter, *The Domi-in(f)o House (model)*, 2002-04.

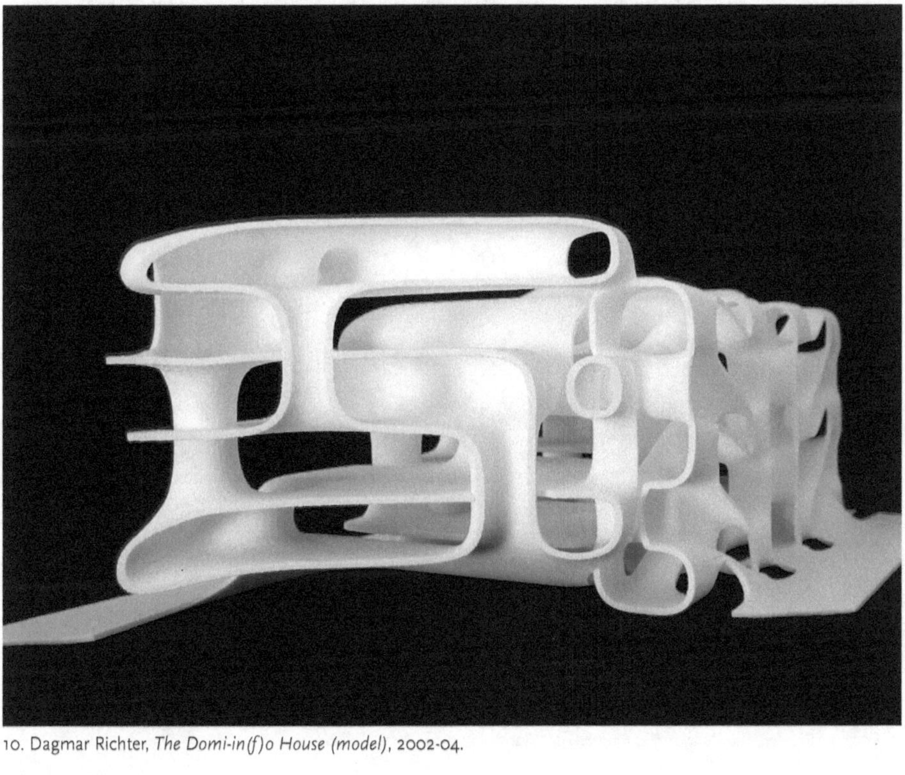

10. Dagmar Richter, *The Domi-in(f)o House (model)*, 2002-04.

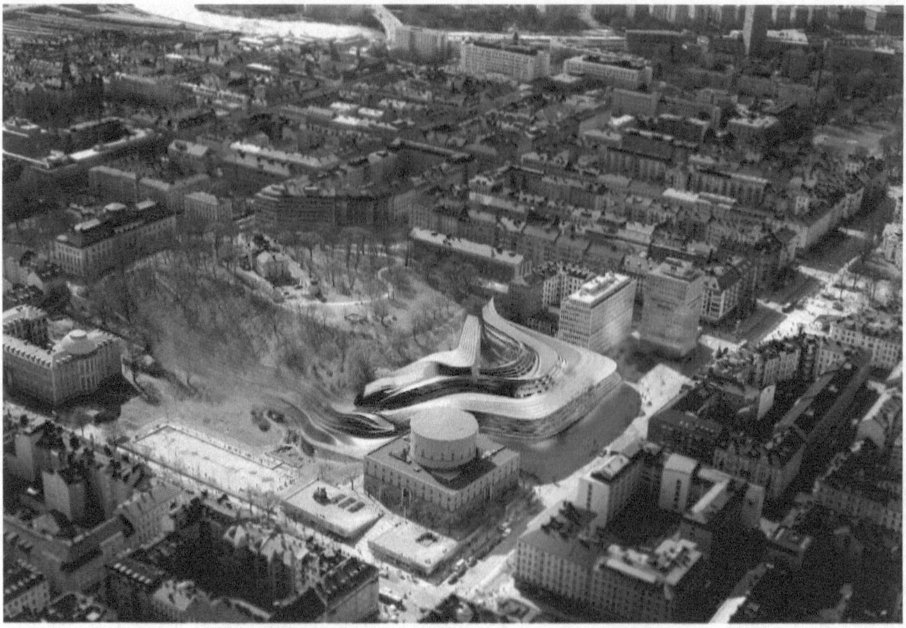

11. Dagmar Richter, *Proposal for the extension of the Stockholm Library competition entry*, 2007.

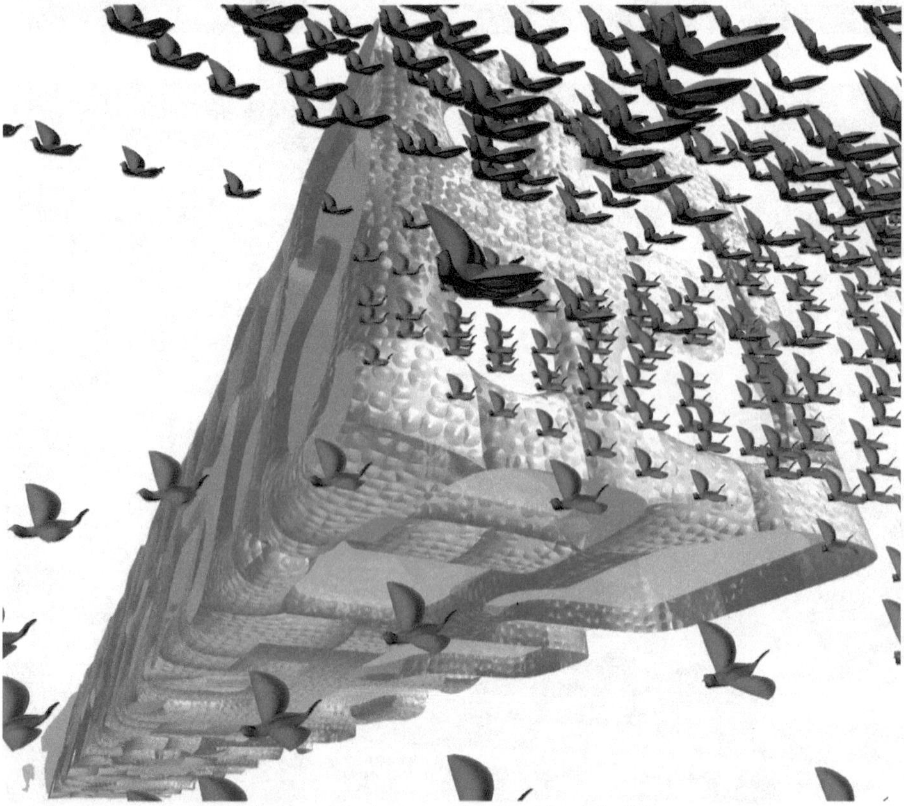

12. Dagmar Richter, *The Domi-in(f)o House: The skyscraper with a 'living' façade for bird*, 2002-04.

EXHIBITING ARCHITECTURE

ARCHITECTURE AS PRACTICE
Exhibiting Herzog and de Meuron

Herzog and De Meuron's exhibition at the Tate Modern—Herzog & de Meuron: An Exhibition 1 June – 29 August 2005—presents twenty-five years of work. The exhibition resists the presentation of heroic photos and perfect models. What is exhibited could be described as the practice of architecture, perhaps more accurately as the exhibition of architecture as a practice. Representation and practice work together.

Jacques Herzog has already responded to the problem posed by architectural representations.

> A building is a building. It cannot be read like a book; it does not have any credits, subtitles or labels like pictures in a gallery. In that sense we are absolutely anti-representational. The strength of our buildings is the immediate visceral impact they have on a visitor.

Expressed in this way Herzog and de Meuron become, on one level, the architects of affect. Once such a positioning is allowed then a specific question emerges; what is it that can be displayed or exhibited in order that affect—Herzog's 'visceral impact'—become the subject of the exhibition? Answering this question necessitates a more general reflection of the image of architecture. After all, what is at stake here is the relationship between architecture and its presentation within and as images.

As images of architecture continue to proliferate, the question of what constitutes the image of architecture prevails. On one level this is a theoretical question generated by the problem of representation. On the other, it is pragmatic and practical. In regards to the latter both magazines and museums engage continually with the presence—thus status—of architecture's image. That engagement in the case of the museum has to resolve itself in a display. Architecture has to be present. While the need is obvious, the question of architecture's image still prevails. Moreover, any answer, while it may appear pragmatic is inescapably bound up with theoretical concerns. The image is, after all, the presentation of architecture; present therefore as architecture's representation.

There is a point at which the theoretical and the pragmatic coincide. The coincidence occurs because the image is always more than mere presence. Any image, be it a photograph, a plan, a model etc., brings with it its own conception of the architectural. Moreover, it is the conception of architecture implicit in the representation that allows for a critical engagement with a given image. Indeed, what structures an exhibition is the coincidence between the theoretical and the pragmatic since exhibitions are not just of images but are also of a given understanding of the architectural. The reciprocity here needs to be noted since that understanding is given within and sustained by the image.

At the same time as it is possible to locate the way this movement operates in the formulation of the architectural exhibition, it is also at work in the differing possibilities within the presentation of architecture's history. For example, to the extent that the history of architecture is understood as the history of the plan then the exhibition of plans is taken to be the presentation of that which is essential to architecture. The same argument will work by extension in terms of an exhibition of materials. The latter is defined by a conception of architecture as defined by the possibilities inherent in materials. Other possibilities exist. In every instance architecture is not a neutral entity that allows itself different forms of presentation. What changes is the conception of the architectural. Any argument against an idealization of architecture—and thus architectural idealism—begins with the recognition not just of a confluence between architecture and image, but that differing images bring different conceptions of the architectural into play.

When Herzog argues that their architecture is concerned with 'visceral impact', what then has to be addressed is what would be involved in an exhibition of architecture as the locus of affect? The immediate answer is that what is defined by such a question is an impossible state of affairs. This is why Herzog defines their work as 'anti-representational'. Precisely because it does not 'represent' then there cannot be a subsequent image of it that would represent it. In other words, what cannot be displayed is that affective quality. It can only be there within the experience of the architecture. This is the problem with which the exhibition at the Tate Modern is constrained to engage. What then of the engagement?

From the now complete Prada Shop and Offices in Tokyo to the earlier and rightly celebrated Ricola-Europe Production and Storage Building in Mulhouse-Brunstatt (France) as well as the Library at the Technical University in Eberswalde (Germany), including London based projects such at the Tate Modern itself, it is difficult to find a project that is not included. How projects are included is the point at issue. Rather than giving priority to any one image—images having a formal presence in relation to models—there is a diverse range of presentation. (As will emerge it is this diversity that becomes the central point.) For any one project there are early models, perhaps even failed models, (or if not failed then certainly abandoned) models of details, models that are experimentation with materials and structural systems drawings and photos are also present. In addition, there are material models ranging in scale and including a 1:1 model. Each project is presented through such a range of different materials and forms—in all there are over 1000 objects—that it is impossible to privilege any one instance.

What emerges as architecture—understood as the locus of architectural experience—arises as a result of the divergent and different practices for which these objects stand. However, it must be emphasized that the architecture is the result. And precisely because it is for Herzog and de Meuron a result there cannot be, experientially, any encounter with it within what is displayed. On display therefore are the diverse sets of practices that will always have a discontinuous relation to a form of finality. If there is anything about the exhibition that may not be completely satisfying it is because the objects have not been aestheticized nor are they illustrative of a continuous process. They are all part of a practice that has its own end game. That end however is not the completing image but the site of affect.

DISPLAYING ARCHITECTURE
Eisenman's Exhibition

Architecture's relation to the museum runs along at least two different axes. In the first instance the relation is defined by acts of construction. Architects design and build museums. The other axis concerns display. Here it is not a question of the design of a given display in any straightforward sense. What is at issue is the display of architecture itself. Hence there will be different questions: how can the museum display architecture? What is an architectural exhibition? On one level the questions are straightforward. The museum for the most part will displays aspects of a given work's construction. Drawings and models are assumed to present architecture. However, they only present it because they are taken to be architecture's representation. The drawing and the model deployed in this way, and with this intent, work with a conception of architecture that has two defining characteristics. The first is that they aim to represent part of the process or envisaged outcome. The outcome and the process are determined by a conception of architecture that is structured by the image. The second is that to the extent that representation and the image are dominant then the architectural effect becomes the relationship between representation and meaning.

The architectural effect is the registration of architecture's presence. In other words, it is the way that presence is registered. The insistence on representation and meaning will structure display in one direction. Architecture's materiality will always be a secondary consideration in relation to representations and meanings. Can a model present materials? Photographs, no matter how they are presented are images of matter rather than the work of matter. And yet, the matter of architecture can never be excluded.

Allowing for matter opens up another way in which there can be the exhibition of architecture. There are, therefore, different questions. How is matter's presence to be exhibited if the centrality of the image—the reduction of matter to its image—is to be distanced and matter reinscribed both as the production of the architectural effect and therefore as the subject to be displayed? How is the exhibition of matter as the display of architecture to be understood?

Matter is, of course, never just present; matter becomes the locus through which techniques come to be articulated. If a start is made with architecture's material presence then there will be a different sense of the architectural effect and therefore a different sense of display. Rather than subordinating matter to its image, and in lieu of a disdaining of matter in the name of meaning, matter, thus material presence, could be taken as the object of display and therefore as the basis of an architectural exhibition. Meaning would be repositioned. It would be the after-effect of the work of matter. There would have been a fundamental shift in the locus of the architectural effect. Meaning would be based on architecture's materiality. However, this should not be seen as arguing for the reduction of architecture to tectonics. The championing of tectonics as an end in itself involves a different form of *naïveté*. Matter is not just material presence. Matter is the site of techniques. Techniques force matter. They give matter its dynamic quality. Furthermore to the extent that techniques involve a relationship between software and the computer then techniques need to be understood as the complex relation between architecture's material presence and the immaterial, though operative quality, of software.

The image and meaning cannot be occluded, however, they need not provide the basis of the architectural effect. Allowing for matter and technique to have primacy orientates that effect in a different direction The display of architecture within the context of a museum dramatizes architecture's complex relation not just to representation—understood as drawing techniques—but also to the way in which architecture comes to be represented as architecture; i.e. the presentation of architectural images. The question that has to be asked therefore concerns the conception of architecture that is present within a given display. The exhibition of the work of Peter Eisenman in the MAK in Vienna gives this question an exacting exigency.[12] Not only is Eisenman's work on display, the

12. The exhibition Barfuss auf weiß glühenden Mauern (Barefoot on White-Hot

question of what counts as that work plays a structuring role in the exhibition. As a consequence, the exhibition is also a detailed investigation of the exhibition of architecture itself.

In general terms architecture's relation to representation figures in a number of different ways. Two of the most predominant concern the image and the model. Images are usually illustrative. Whether it be a book, journal or magazine the image is intended to illustrate. At one extreme it illustrates an argument and therefore grounds it. At the other it is simply illustrates. In such a context illustration is no more than the photograph of a building. While architecture cannot escape a direct engagement with the way it is represented, the question of the extent to which the image of architecture has to be no more than an illustration is an important one. Is it possible to move from an illustrative image to a generative one? The same question will pertain to the model. Models are conventionally used to represent the architectural project. This particular conception of representation however is not to be understood in terms of material possibility. Nor moreover does the project's presentation enact the relationship between geometry and materiality. The model stands for the building. It becomes its image. While working to scale it does no more than illustrate the project. The presence of this limitation means that this restriction—a reduction of the model to illustration—can be questioned. With that questioning another possibility will emerge. In sum, could the model be other than illustrative? Inherent in this question is the possibility that the representation—here the model—could be productive rather than a passive illustration.

These questions acknowledge the inter-articulation of architecture and representation. They do so, however, in a way that allows for an opening, one where the status of the representation can be interrogated. While that interrogation could take a discursive form, within the context of the MAK it is present as an architectural exhibition. In terms of the structure of the display, Eisenman has introduced a 'grid' into the Exhibition Hall at the MAK.

A series of white boxes (or cubes) mark the presence of the 'grid'. The boxes gesture as much to the column as they do to the tradition of the museum as 'white cube'. In regards to the former what is recalled is the structural relationship between column and grid. Metonymically, architecture is staged. In regard to the latter, as the columns are only 2.65 metres in diameter the assumptions

Walls) was on show at the MAK in Vienna December 15 2004 until May 2005.

inherent in the equation of museum with the white cube are productively explored. The exploration is architectural. Scale ruins the pretensions of the white cube. In so doing, what is demonstrated is the way in which the white cube sanctioned a display of art that had a determining effect not just on what counted as art but on the way such an identification was inextricably bound up with the question of display. There is an implicit levelling effect that the equation of white cube and museum enacts. The simple destruction of that equation would have amounted to no more than the nihilism of its refusal. The work of scale, if only as a beginning, signals the presence of a different quality. Destruction and a type of dis-ordering work together with and as strategies of creation.[13] That quality is however neither merely discursive (accompanying the exhibition as an argument that would be irrelevant to the exhibition's material presence.) Nor is it decorative. It is present as a simple addition. What could be understood as the deconstruction of the assumptions at work in the equation of white cube and museum—a deconstruction staged initially by scale—is the operative quality within these column boxes.

What then of the display? Any answer to this question has to begin with the recognition that the exhibition has as its intention an overview of Eisenman's work from the early House projects to the most recent competition entries and works under constructions. In total, almost 35 years of projects are displayed. The question returns: what is displayed? While an example won't really suffice, it will work to stage the exhibition's concerns. One of the works that remains pivotal within Eisenman's overall development is the Wexner Center for the Visual Arts in Columbus Ohio. The usual documentation of this building consists of photographs of the rebuilt tower present on the south façade. And yet, fundamental to the overall conception and execution of the building was the way two different grid systems began to redefine the site. Integral to that redefinition is the way the relationship between the grid systems works to locate both circulation and volume. If there was an element of the building that enacted this redefinition it was the scaffolding that is projected across and through the building. While a photograph of the now extant building will present the scaffolding's image—a presentation held by the constraints of illustration—the registration of that which endures as

13. See the discussion of 'dis-ordering' in 'Visual Memory: Whiteread and Eisenman'.

essential to the project's generation is only ever present as an element in a photograph. The problematic element within the display of the Wexner Center is twofold. On the hand there has to be a form of presentation that resists the assimilating effect—and thus the banalizing inevitability—of the photograph, while at the same time moving what is to be displayed from a logic of illustration to one in which abstraction predominates. Such a move allows for the introduction both of that which had a generative effect, though in a way that would allow it to retain that possibility for a future project. In other words, the move is from a presentation bound by illustration to one structured by what could be described as the logic of the diagram. While the choice may appear stark—and as with all seemingly stark opposition it admits of points of overlap—what is at work here is a distinction between the passivity of an illustration—one which remains passive precisely because it is at the same time precise and yet empty—and the dynamic quality of the diagram. The latter, in resisting the logic of representation stages the building in a complex way. The complexity is at work in the image's abstraction. Abstraction in such a context is defined as what carries potential. Consequently, it is what allows for the generation of future representations.

The display of the Wexner Center, almost inevitably, is an element of the scaffolding. However, the question that has to be asked of the element's exhibition has to concern the question of what architecturally is there to be seen in such a display. In sum, how does an element of the scaffolding display the Wexner Center? Posed the other way, the question concerns the reluctance (perhaps refusal) to equate the building with the illustrative image. What then? The answer to the question of display hinges on what counts as architecture. While an illustration is clearly illustrative of architecture, what the illustration cannot make present is a project's operative dimension. The operative cannot be conflated with the tectonic—such a move is no more than naïve materialism that in the end becomes a shambling form of empiricism. On the contrary, the operative is inherent in any account of the generative logic allowing for the building. Precisely because the operative has a diagrammatic quality it will always have an extension that is greater than any one instance of its enactment.

What is on display makes demands. Eisenman's exhibition has a compelling quality precisely because of the intellectual demands it makes. The thirty column boxes—each of which presents a project or building—continue to pose the question of architecture's display. This does not occur in a way that resists particularity. The contrary is the case. Each column box can be identified with a particular project. The question of architecture is always articulated through the particular and not posed in terms of mere generality. Architecture, therefore, has never been more emphatically on display. The move from the illustrative image to the image as diagram—a move from a concern with representation to one governed by the operative and therefore potentiality—overcomes the reduction of architecture to its illustration by displaying the demands of the question of architecture.

RESEARCHING ARCHITECTURE
Recent Projects by Diller + Scofidio

As a world in which research is only thought to be viable if it is legitimated by grant applications exercises a greater hold on academic and intellectual life, the possibility of another form of research becomes a more insistent question. That question is one that can only be posed once there is an effective separation of experimentation and confirmation. In addition, this has to be coupled to overcoming the cynicism that would deny the reality of real discovery. What these possibilities allude to is a space where research and experimentation will have a different type of presence. And yet, the question of research is far from simple. In addition, the question of what counts as research in architecture is highly contested. There is no doubt that architecture can engage productively with conceptual art. However, conceptual art is not architectural research. There is therefore the real need to distinguish between significant architectural moments within conceptual art—Gordon Matta Clark's House Projects are a clear instance– and research that takes the centrality of form making, for example, as its object. The questions return. What is research in architecture? Within architecture what counts as experimentation?

If these questions were addressed to poetry then the answer would be straightforward. It would be to use the elements of poetry—its own extended vocabulary—in ways that caused these elements to be rethought, or even to be given a life that had not previously been envisaged. In other words, the elements of poetry would be both added to and transformed in the process. What happens when such demands are made of architecture? Such a question is, of course, the one that defines the ambit of experimentation and research. Moreover, it locates the place where recent work by Diller and Scofidio can be located. However, that work is not just experimental. As their recent exhibition at the Whitney Museum in New York (which took place between March 1 – May 25 2003) indicates, there are projects in the process of being built as opposed to ones which, even when realized, remain at the experimental level. The question is how is the relationship between the two to be understood? Rather than try and do justice to such an extensive body of material, two projects will be taken. Of their recent works the two which have attracted the most attention are the Blur Building (2002) and the Eyebeam Museum of Art and Technology. The latter, an ostensibly architectural project was intended to be located in Manhattan. The former, an experiment, was completed and used as part of Swiss Expo2002.

The Blur Building, which was located on Lake Neuchatel in Switzerland, utilized a tensegrity structural form first developed by Buckminster Fuller. The structure incorporated a complex computer controlled weather station linked to a pump system. The activation of the system operating through 31,5000 nozzles could create a fog atmosphere. The detail of the project would seem to militate any description of it as experimental. However the reason why, in this context, that it become possible to describe it is as experimental is not because it is yet to be built. There was a construction. Nor, because it fell outside any functional concerns. There were clear functional constraints all of which worked effectively. Indeed, what allows them to work *was* an integrated system involving, computers, a pumping systems and a complex built environment. Its experimental nature is to be found elsewhere. While a great deal of interest lay in its apparent refusal of the spectacle and therefore in the capacity of the work to evoke 'nothing', there is an additional element that needs to be noted. The addition is the way, within the work, the divide between the material and the immaterial is slowly eroded. The effect of the fog, the bodily sense of an enclosure whose materiality is both present yet evanescent, does more than open up the question of materials. It shows in what way a concern with materials and their relation to bodies and the body's expectations—especially those whose materiality is more nuanced and here it would not matter whether it was fog or surface defined by porosity rather than solidity—can be investigated within architecture. The scripting of material/body relations is not meant to have direct entailments. The Blur Building is not meant to proliferate. It is not a prototype. If anything it is a diagram. It opens possibilities defined by the potentialities that the object contains. Its presence as a site of experimentation, therefore, is inextricably bound up with this diagrammatic status. Straightforwardly, what this means is that it has a generative quality. That quality is there as a potential; in the futural possibilities that this investigation of the relationship between the immaterial and the material may have on form, generation and the positioning of bodies in space.

On one level The Eyebeam Museum is a different entity altogether. What is projected here is the realization of a complex program that is brought about by what the building's geometry makes possible. The brief necessitate that the Museum function as much as an exhibition centre as a workshop or atelier for new technology. While integrated, there needs to be two buildings. More than that, the actual building must allow for the technological innovations occurring within it to then be incorporated as part of the building's infrastructure. As a number of a commentators have pointed out this introduces a stark shift in priorities. Instead of privileging a volume that permits reprogramming, it is the actual architecture that will make this possible. The continual slide and intersection of the buildings within the overall structure yields openings for the insertion, this incorporation, of technological developments. Loading bearing operates on the vertical as well as on the horizontal axis. The double programming demands of the brief are met by the operation of the architecture. Not only are exhibitions spaces opened up. It is also the case that the atelier areas have surfaces allowing for the continual redeployment of the technical innovations that will arise within them. In addition, the co-presence of two buildings within a building means that points of intersection occur such that a shift in program or a blurring of programs results. This is brought about in the first instance by the overall geometry of the structure. Secondly, it occurs because of the specific nature of the materials used. Instead of the univocity of form follows function, or its mirror opposite where form—as blob—can accommodate any function, a movement that never really took material into consideration, here complex form allows for a complexity of function. Both types of complexity are occasioned by the nature of the materials used. The materials in question are as much concerned with load bearing as they are with what the atelier surfaces will allow.

What distinguishes this project from the Blur Building is its singularity. Singularity in contemporary architecture can be defined by the tight relationship between, geometry, materials and function. As what materials will allow becomes more nuanced and hence more intricate, as specific buildings can realize complex programs because of the particular way materials and geometry can be related, buildings understood either as generic types or as prototypes for future buildings vanishes. Singularity emerges because buildings contain a potential that is internal to their construction. Their future lies within the way their construction allows for adaptation and transformation. (The latter then become part of the 'function'. This defines the way the relationship between exhibition spaces and the workshops is envisaged in the Eyebeam Museum.) The potential of such buildings is not external. In other words, they are not prototypes, let alone diagrams. The construction of singularity is one of the most significant ways in which modern architecture appears. Finally, if it is possible to define the locus of experimentation and research in architecture, a start can be made by concentrating on the opening, perhaps the space, created by the relationship between the diagrammatic and the singular.

THE STANDARDS OF THE *NON STANDARD*

Exhibitions of architecture can be significant occasions. Rather than the predictable display of images and models they can attempt to stage architecture's current concerns. This is especially the case when the rationale behind the display aims at situating innovation rather than presenting either simple historical continuities or celebrating mere novelty. Such has to be the point of departure for any analysis of the exhibition, *Architecture Non Standard,* curated by Frédéric Migayrou, and held at the Centre Pompidou in Paris between 10 December, 2003 and 1 March, 2004. Included in the exhibition is work by some of the most innovative studios and practitioners working today. Of those in the exhibition notable inclusions are Asymptote, dECOI Architects, DR_D, Greg Lynn FORM, KOL/MAC Studio, NOX, Objectile, Odsterhuis.nl, Servo and UN Studio.

Unlike other important exhibitions that aimed to capture a fundamental shift in how architectural practice and theory has occurred, this exhibition attempts to provide real historical and theoretical unity. Rather than simply assuming that recent developments in animation software have generated specific forms of architectural practice, the project is to provide those developments with a historical and theoretical context. However, the context is not given by arguing that these developments are part of a simple, linear progression within architectural history. On the contrary, the curatorial strategy is that the context occurs and can be created precisely because recent architectural innovations allow it. In other words, the strategy is one that seeks to construct a history of the present, rather than construing the present moment as no more than a simple occurrence within a movement of historical time understood as inherently sequential. In addition, the curatorial strategy—and it has to be acknowledged that it is an artfully conceived one aided by Philippe Morel's development of a scheme for situating the projects with the Galerie Sud of the Centre Pompidou—involves more than the simple presentation of pictures and models.

Positioned within the exhibition are large warping panels of images organized under the following headings: Figures, Mathematical Objects, Lines, Impressions (*Empreintes*), Inflexions, Ribbons. Each large panel of images works in two ways. On the one hand they orientate the viewer and play a role in directing movement within the exhibition. The encounter with an actual given display of a specific architect's work is mediated. Secondly, what really matters is what is doing this mediating. The images displayed on large panels are visually coherent. It is that very coherence that does the work. For example, the images grouped under the heading 'Inflections' allow similarities to be noted between Gaudi, Freyssionet, Scharoun, Breuer, Jacobsen and Lundy amongst others. Images of individual works create networks of associations. Rather than resolving questions, the presence of these networks allows a type of contextualism to be created, one that undoes the easy compartmentalization of architectural history, thereby demanding a revision of such terms as modernism. This way of creating a context—one defined by the present—has the important effect of robbing the present of its novelty. Reciprocally, of course, it thereby raises as a question how relation and lineage are to be understood. This mode of display needs to be situated in relation to Migayrou's own theorization of the 'non standard' in his closely argued catalogue essay.[14] (A catalogue which also contains an important article by Mark Burry, whose final questioning of what image is adequate to present the non standard touches on the problematic status of the image today. A status that should not lead towards iconoclasm, but to a renewal of methods of interpretation and thus the development of another theory of the architectural image.)

The origin of the term 'non standard' is the work of the mathematician Abraham Robinson. Fundamental to the overall argument is overcoming the separation of a mathematical realm and a realm of matter. Replacing that opposition is an approach

14. Frédéric Migayrou, 'Les ordres non standard', in *Architectures non standard*, Editions de Centre Pompidou, Paris, 2003, pp. 26-33. (All translations are my own.)

delimited by morphogenesis, which in Migayrou's reformulation of aspects of René Thom's work involves 'a formalization, *a priori*, of the mutations of matter'.[15] Once there is a continuity or a confluence between mathematics and matter, then rather than a geometry that is always exterior to production, geometry and production need to be thought of as occurring together. (This point, to which it will be essential to return, will allow for a differentiation to be made between the projects. Since each of the projects differ in terms of how this intrinsic relation is both understood and enacted.) The strategy of the exhibition is to show the ways that mathematics and architecture, both reconceived in terms of the 'non standard', coincide in the present conjuncture. Once a set-up of this nature is accepted as a point of departure, different issues of importance arise. For example, the question is not the move to form as such, but an understanding of form—architecture's formal, hence material instantiation—as a singularity. Rather than form being the end result of a process, once morphogenesis defines movement then, in Migayrou's formulation: 'Form becomes a morphogenetic, *a priori*, the forms chosen in order to instantiate (*incarner*) architecture only being the definition of a state of singularity in a continuum of perpetual evolution'.[16] In fact, this is a straightforward issue. To the extent that animation software is integral to the process of design then the question is always going to be how a given moment will be understood as no longer simply diagrammatic, but as architectural form. Singularity provides a way into the different projects. All of them raise the issue of the nature of their formal presence. In its simplest form, the question will always concern the nature of what, seen either on the screen or as a model, is architecture.

The setting of these works, by providing a coherent context, brings with it an attendant risk; the risk is simply that by the provision of a form of coherence, in particular one established on the level of the image, then all of these works could be viewed as no more than different versions of the 'same' approach. While it is clear that there is a similar point of departure, it is also true that between the projects important differences can be located. Two need to be noted. The first concerns the relationship between diagrams and materials. In general terms, one of the most exacting questions raised by these projects concerns their material

15. Migayrou, 'Les ordres non standard', p. 26.
16. Migayrou, 'Les ordres non standard', p. 32.

realization. The evaluation of any architecture that originates in the diagram is the envisaged relation it has to the question of material presence. The second involves the use of the non standard to begin to explore questions of program.

Real distinctions can be drawn, for example, between the work of Greg Lynn Form and Asymptote on the one hand and NOX (Lars Spuybroek) on the other. In regards to the former, the geometry of the diagrams is realized without any form of mediation. Lynn's Embryological Houses become a clear case in point. The geometry is always internal to the software and never a quality of the matter (the materials) in which it would come to be realized. It is as though a new type of ideality enters precisely because questions of materiality do not figure as a site of architectural investigation and thus experimentation. The work of NOX has to be distinguished radically from such procedures. Lars Spuybroek's formal investigation of the potentiality of materials opens up a fundamentally different path. His construction of material investigations—based in part on the work of Frei Otto—as analogue-computer model which, through a process of digitalization means that the process starts from materials and ends with them. Lynn, and he is not alone here, evinces within the context of this exhibition no real interest in the potential of materials. Materiality does not emerge as a site of investigation in its own right.

Some of the most important projects that are driven by programmatic concerns involve strategic operations that work to undo the strict opposition between the public and the private. Secondly, there are those whose work is not undertaken on the level of the building but on the urban scale. While there are important affinities between this latter form of work and the emergent discipline of landscape urbanism, in this context the interplay between the non standard as mode of analysis and representation takes precedence. If it is fundamental to the project of the non standard is to allow differences and discontinuities to be bound up with forms of continuity—in other words, it will involve a line that distributes discontinuous elements—then such a procedure will be fundamental to a rethinking of actual architectural and social oppositions.

The two architectural practices that exemplify both a concern with the urban, as well as an investigation of the public and the private are UN Studio. (Ben van Berkel) and DR_D (Dagmar Richter). Two projects that are directly concerned with the urban are UN Studio's Las Palmas Bridge project in which the continuities of flows allows the individual elements to emerge and DR_D's investigation of Waterford. In regards to issues pertaining to the public and the private of particular note are SERVO's Lobby Ports Hotel and DR_D's Maison Dom-In(f)o. The force of the latter is that, what was an originally literally discontinuous structure—Le Corbusier's Maison Domino—through its digitalization becomes a continuity that is then able to generate different discontinuous elements. The freedom that was thought to be there in the domino frame is investigated and more fully realized by establishing a generative continuity that is not restricted formally. The absence of formal restriction is the mark of the effective presence of the non standard.

Overall the exhibition demands a response. The challenge resides in the proposition that the conventions of history and theory are no longer adequate to the task. Rethinking contemporary architecture in terms of the non standard is not mere speculation. It has to be construed as a response to the needs created by what forms and informs architectural practice today.

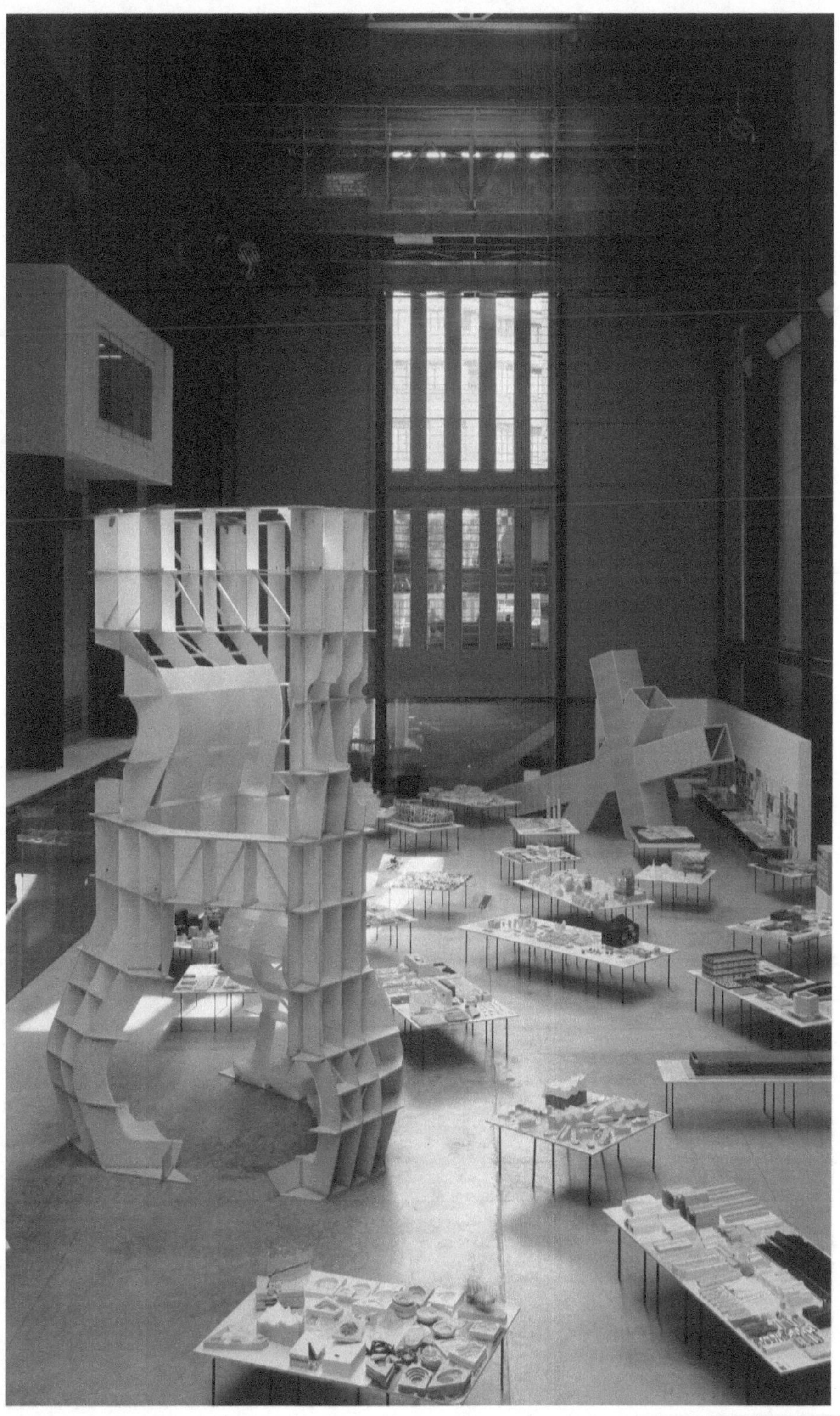

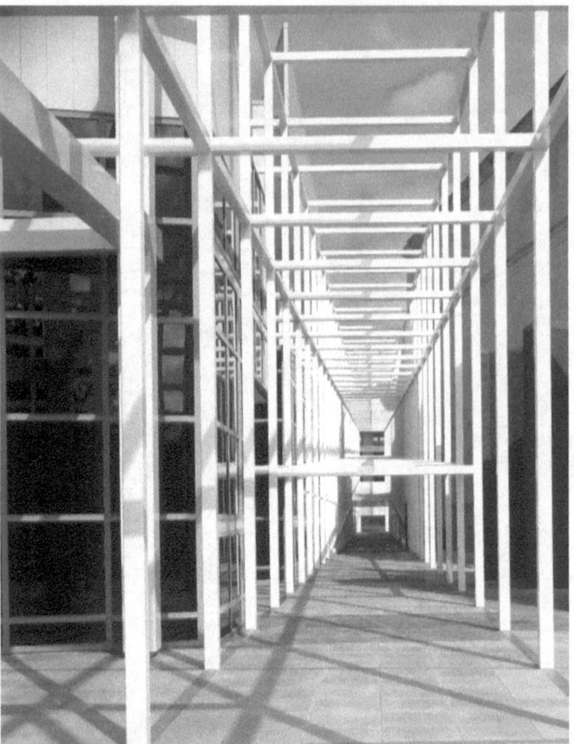

13. Herzog and De Meuron, *Exhibition at the Tate Modern*, 2005 (previous page).
14. Peter Eisenman, *Wexner Center for the Visual Arts, Ohio State University*, 1989.

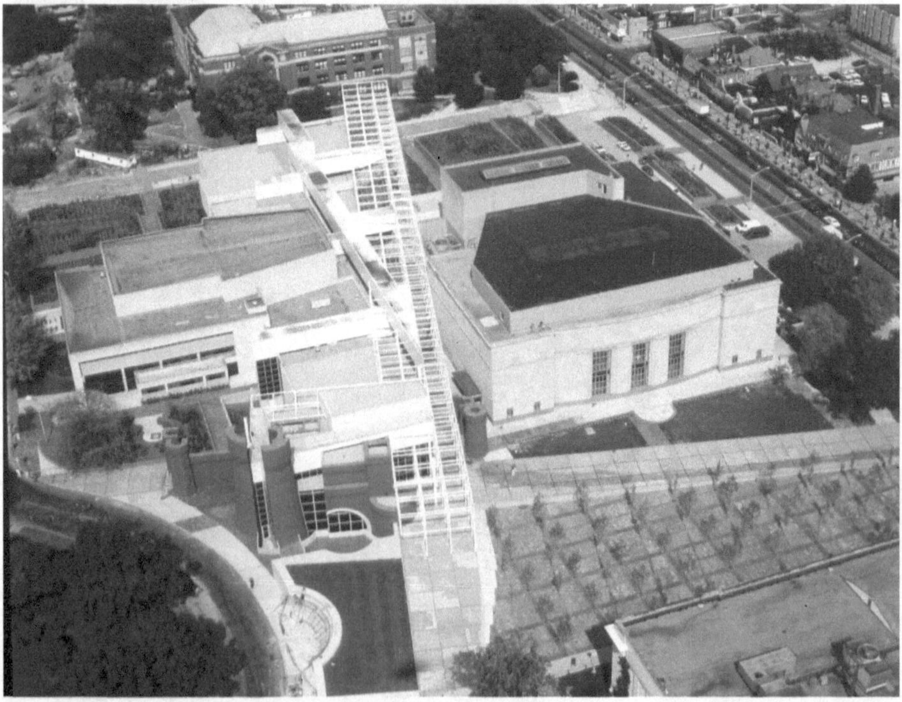

15. Peter Eisenman, *Wexner Center for the Visual Arts, Ohio State University*, 1989.

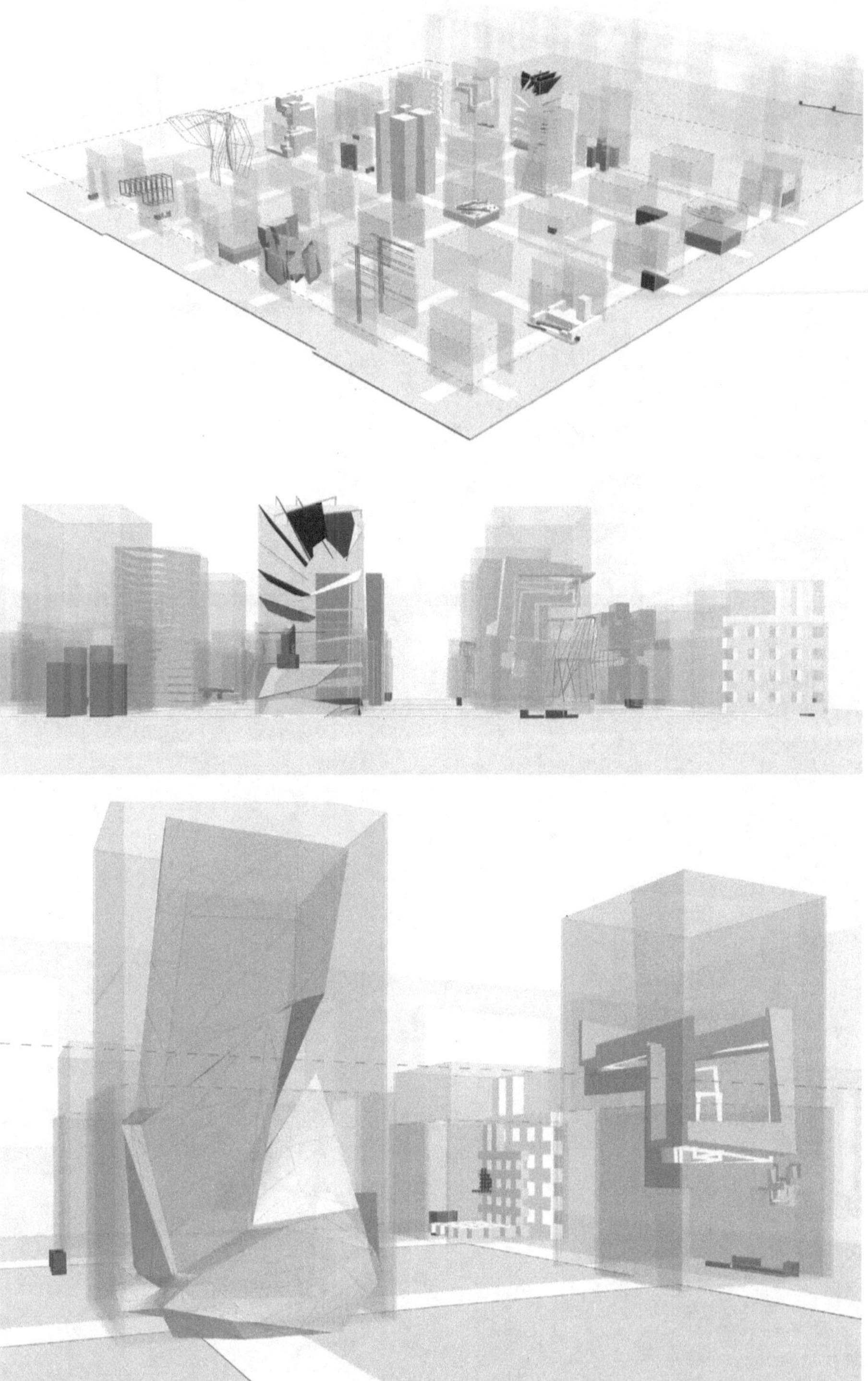

23-25. Peter Eisenman, *Barefoot on White-Hot Walls (Exhibition at the MAK)*, 2004-5.

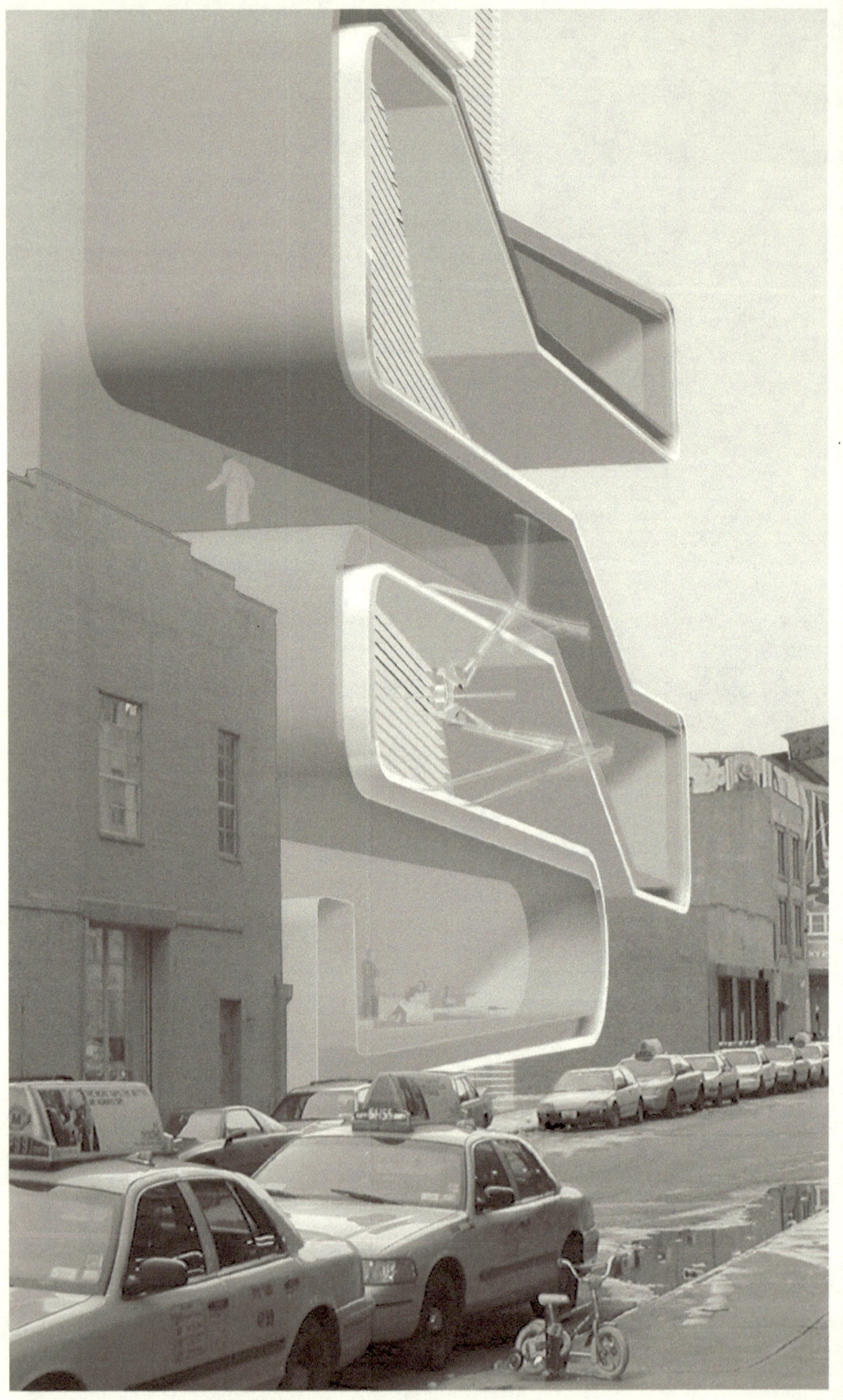

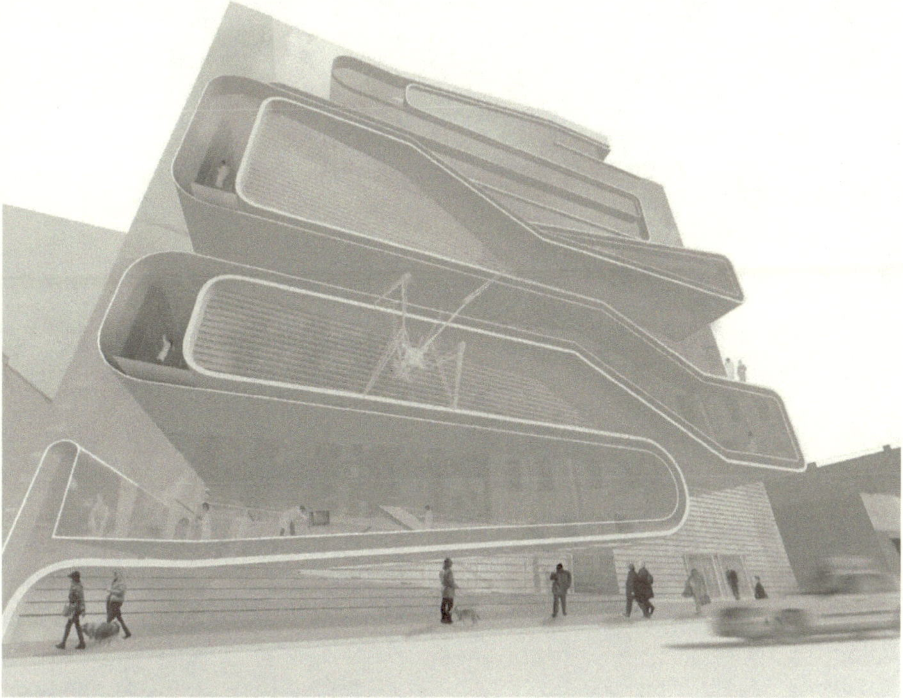

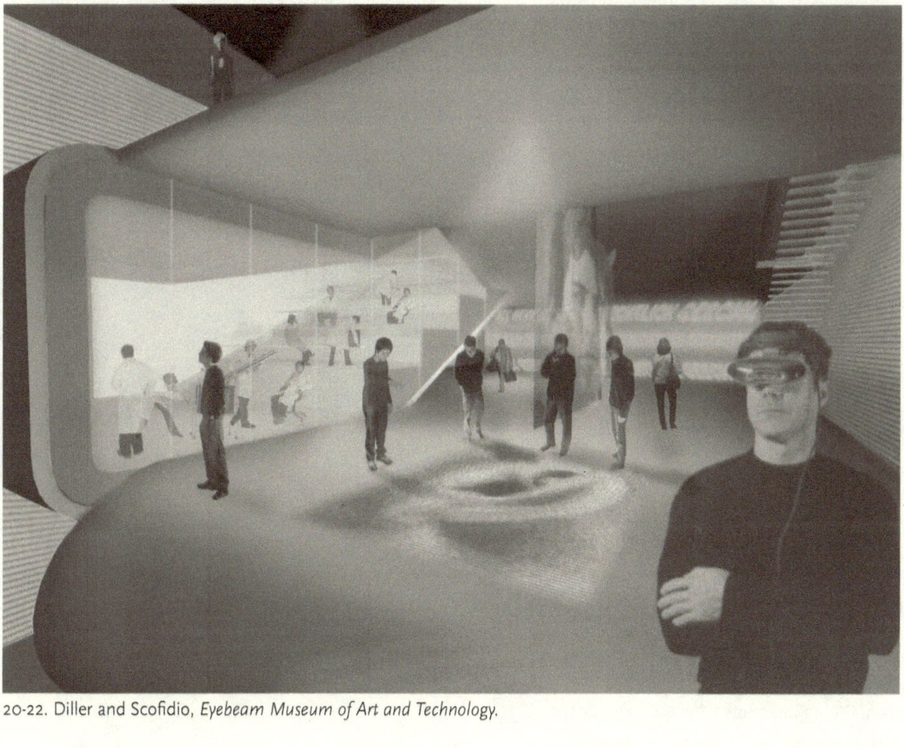

20-22. Diller and Scofidio, *Eyebeam Museum of Art and Technology.*

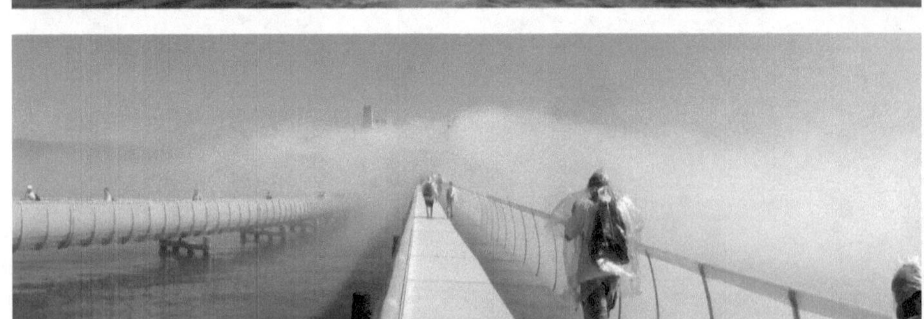

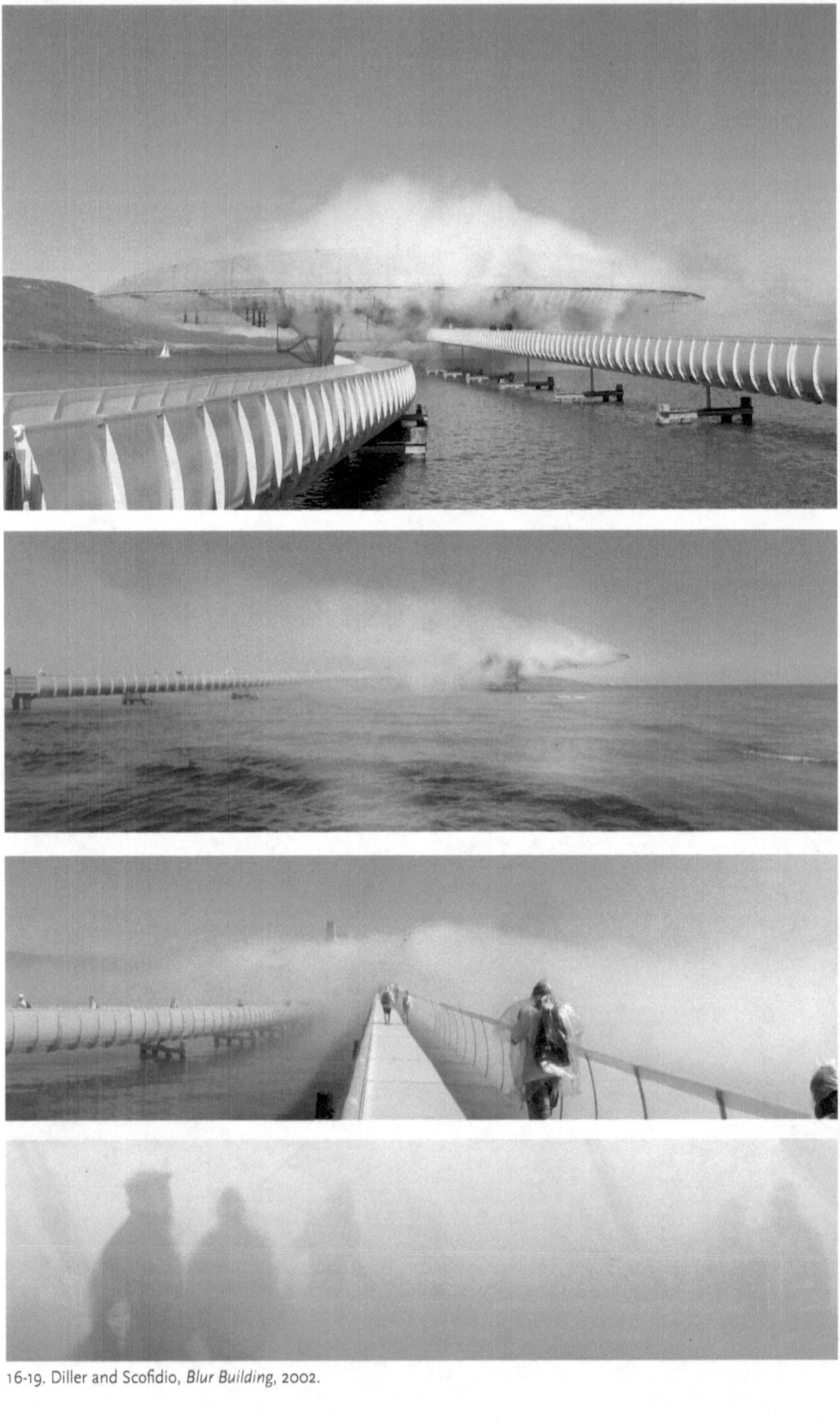

16-19. Diller and Scofidio, *Blur Building*, 2002.

PAINTING

MYTH AND HISTORY
Anselm Kiefer's Aperiatur Terra

Both architecture and art can be sites of memory. Modes of remembering, and therefore, the way the work of memory occurs will in each case be different. Nonetheless, in certain instances works situated in the present remember. Remembering need be neither complacent nor nostalgic. Daniel Libeskind's The Jewish Museum Berlin (1999) is a perfect instance of a project that maintains its architectural integrity and yet which also allows for what can be called *present remembrance*.[15] The latter being the form of memory demanded by the concerns of the present. While architecture's relation to memory and the complex process of memorialization endure as a constant prompt, art's relation to memory is a more complex question. The work of the German painter Anselm Kiefer allows the question of art's relation to *present remembrance* to be posed. Precisely because what is at play here is the relationship between history, memory and the image it is essential to begin with time.

Paul Klee's well-known riposte to Lessing's separation of time and space, was to insist that space was always temporal. If that temporality is enlarged to include history, then it will incorporate one of the problems that has confronted continually the project of painting; namely, how can history figure within a practice constrained by the single image. It is vital to be precise here. The question does not concern the presence of historical subjects. Rather, history in this instance is linked to a conception of place, perhaps even of geography. Once place is understood as the site of history then landscape will have ceded its usual determination to another conception of the ground.

15. I have offered a sustained account of this term both generally and in relation to Libeskind's museum in my *Present Hope: Philosophy, Architecture, Judaism*, Routledge, London, 1997.

One possible way to allow time into painting is the attempt to capture a moment. Manet's *Woman Reading* (1878/9) or Tom Roberts' *The Summer Morning Tiff* (1886) convey an instant. Meaning is drawn into the image consequently the image will always hold more than the instant conveyed. Nonetheless time is linked to moments. Manet's painting is of a woman in the public sphere absorbed by the changing record of public events, the newspaper. Roberts' use of perspective captures the moment after the lovers have separated. Her stance is forlorn, and he is proceeding into the background. The painting is defined by distance and immediacy. Both paintings hold the viewer through the presentation of the moment. Moments register history on the level of meaning. However, history is not a sequence of moments.

Once the separation of history and moments (the latter being the register of time defined by chronology) is allowed then the question of the presentation of history within painting becomes more exacting. Not only is there the historical situation within which the paintings are situated, there is also the way that situation becomes art work. For German painting in the wake of the Second World War, and especially after the Holocaust the situation, while stark, was clear. However, what was equally as apparent was the necessity for art to work within this opening. Art and history would coincide within paintings. Their coincidence would be the paintings.

It is not difficult to see Kiefer's work of the 70s and throughout the 80s as defined by this project. Works such as *Nero Paints* (1974), *Iconoclastic Controversy*, (1980) and *Icarus—March Sands* (1981) all concern art's relation to the ground of history. Indeed, in all these works the landscape is present as a marked ground. The marking of the ground by human activity is history's visible inscription onto the land. While the inscribed presence of either the simple palette, or more provocatively a winged palette into these works gives art a presence that hovers above the ground, what is of equal concern is art's relation to that ground. The essential point here is that hovering is not transcendence. The ground as the site of history is marked in advance as art's concern. What always matters, therefore, is a relation. The question of relationality is given its most emphatic expression in Kiefer's work in his painting *Your Golden hair Margarete* (1981).

This painting—and it is one of a number on this 'theme'—evokes both in title and detail Paul Celan's 1954 poem *Todesfuge*

(*Death Fugue*). Celan's poem is perhaps the most famous literary reflection on the Holocaust and specifically on the complex interplay between the land, mythology and history. Celan's concerns are German. When Kiefer evokes the poem in his painting he does so initially by placing straw on the canvas as though it were strands of golden hair. Written on to the canvas are the words from the poem that are also the work's title, 'Dein Goldenes Haar, Margarethe'. As these words are repeated throughout the poem the precise reference is left open. That openness is not the question. What matters is the way the interplay of words, the 'hair' and the ploughed field, i.e. the earth (recalling for a moment that one of the most harrowing words in Celan's poem is 'Erde' ['earth']) work together. Within these works history figures.

As he progressed Kiefer become more concerned with myth. While his work had always deployed mythic figures; that use was continually mediated by a concern with the place of history. Myth and history worked together. The materiality of the surface, an almost literal manifestation of the earth's materiality, was traversed as much by the mythic as by the historical. Myth worked in the service of history. In *The Birth of Tragedy*, Nietzsche had used the mythic figure of Dionysus to upset Germany's complacent relation to Greece. For Nietzsche, certain mythic figures contained the power to demythologize. Nonetheless, myth brings with it a fundamental instability. In sum, the problem with the recourse to myth is that it can become just that. As myth begins to predominate a concern with history as a placed occurrence is effaced. The only way history could be written back in would be in terms of its reconstruction as myth.

The exhibition of Kiefer's work at the Art Gallery of New South Wales Aperiatur Terra can be interpreted in exactly these terms.[16] While many of the stylistic motifs that have characterized his projects since the 70s are there—strong material presence, the carving of the earth either by plough or the creation of roads, writing on the painting's surface, etc.—they are being deployed for a different end. In many of the works that make up the exhibition, figures from Greek mythology have interconnected with defining aspects of Christianity. While this may have the effect of equating Christianity with mythology, what it does in addition is remove the work from a relation to the present. Mythology has become truly

16. The exhibition took place at the Art Gallery of New South Wales in Sydney from May 19, 2007 until July 29, 2007.

transcendent. It is as though the paintings stage two orders. There is, however, more involved.

The work from which the exhibition takes its title—Aperiatur Terra et Germinet Salvatorem (2005-6)—comes from a line in Isaiah. The English translation of the line is as follows: 'Let the earth be opened and bring forth a saviour....drop down dew, ye heavens from above and let the clouds rain down the just'. Again the title is written across the top of this massive painting (2800 x 7600 mm). Moreover, scale, the use of heavy material to present the ground and the marking of the ground recall earlier works. That recall is reinforced by the addition of flowers. Now the flowers have a different presence. The Book of Isaiah to which reference is made is from the Old Testament rather than the Hebrew Bible. The line in Latin occurs within the service on Palm Sunday. However, Palm Sunday is already connected to an array of flowers in its German presence as 'Blumensonntag'.

The move in this painting—and it is repeated in others making up the exhibition—is not to religion or mythology in any straightforward sense. In fact these are demanding paintings that refuse a simple explanation. They stage the movement away from the interplay of art and the ground of history to art's complex appropriation of the temporality of mythology. No longer is there a concern with the present and thus an attempt to use art to work through German history. Within these paintings what hope there is lives on in the repetitive ritual of myth. Redemption has lost the political measure that Walter Benjamin would have given it. If there is a genuine politics of hope then it is linked to the possibility of an opening that is a restaging that falls beyond the hold of prediction. The changing seasons in which flowers bloom, then wither and die only to be born again is the temporal structure in which nothing changes. This is the temporality of myth. A temporality that stands opposed to history.

Within architecture Libeskind's Jewish Museum allowed for a link between architecture and hope—more accurately present hope—because it allowed the concerns of the present to set the measure. In so doing there is a formal presence that refused the demands of either continuity or cyclical repetition. As history gives way to myth Kiefer's paintings lose their sense of engagement. Rather than sites of engagement they become sites of reverence. As such art work becomes contemplative and its hold merely aesthetic.

ART THAT MATTERS
Hawley's Work

1.

With any work of art there is an inescapable and insistent question: What is being seen? If the question is answered such that the response attributes to the work its own power of production then what is seen is what the work evidences, i.e. the complex relation between materiality and production. However, what often predominates is another form of response one in which all that seems to matter are forms of identification. As such, the answer to the opening question would be the identification and contextualization of the work's title. The presupposition would be that naming and contextualizing the work, the title being the name, accounted for what is seen. Such an approach does not just fail to respond to the work, as significantly it refuses the potential within the complex relationship between art and writing. While titles will always figure, to the extent that there is a shift in orientation such that identification is incorporated within the position in which art is defined in terms of work and thus one where production is central, any response to the question of the work's presentation becomes radically different. Once that move is made and even though writing will still be constrained by the necessity to describe, writing will have become linked to a fundamentally different project. Writing becomes criticism because its concern is with the way a given work works as art.

By focusing on production, art's material presence is given centrality. Emphasizing materials, however, should not be understood merely in terms of the technical dimension of art works. There is a different sense of work involved. (Hence, a different philosophical approach to the question—what is art?) If the interplay between title, description and the technical were taken as ends in themselves this would then mean that the term 'work' entailed an already present form of completion. As though the work is over once the actual work—painting, sculpture, etc.—is named (titled) and thus the task of writing became description or contextualization. Within such a frame of reference work is no more than a substantive. Eschewing this form of nominalism, one in which the object is equated with its already completed form, necessitates as indicated, another way of construing the relation between art and writing. The basis of this difference does not involve abandoning the object in the name of an extra material dimension. Equally, it does not necessitate the introduction of either the subjective or the gesturally historical into a concern with art. This other relation opens up to the extent that the connection between work and completion is distanced such that it no longer determines the project of writing.

What emerges with this distancing is a different sense of work. In lieu of other determinations work is then allowed an active or productive quality. While the formulation appears tautological it is, nonetheless, essential to recognize that intrinsic to art works is their capacity to work. In place of the static and the substantive centrality is given to what can be described as the object's workful nature and thus to its active or dynamic quality. As a consequence what insists is the question of the way the work works. What needs to be noted in this context is threefold. In the first instance, it is the move from the substantive to the dynamic. In the second, there is the necessity to replace completion with a productive sense of work and finally the necessity to rethink art's material presence as itself involving process. Occasioned by the last element is the need to reposition a concern with materiality. Instead of the simple evocation of matter, once it is rethought in terms of the continuity of process—production and materiality as always connected—matter will become 'mattering'. (A term to be clarified below.)[17] All of these elements pertain to art work. Moreover, they are all demanded by the claims made on writing, and thus the project of interpretation, by the work of David Hawley. This is not to argue that he is unique among contemporary artists. Rather, it is to argue that his

17. I have discussed this aspect of painting in 'The Matter of a Materialist Philosophy of Art: Bataille's Manet' in my *Style and Time: Essays on the Politics of Appearance*, Northwestern University Press, Chicago, 2006, pp. 124-138. See in addition my *Disclosing Spaces: On Painting*, Clinamen Press, Manchester 2004.

work does not just take place in a specific location, namely painting in the era of digital reproducibility, it does so in an exemplary and affirmative way. Any encounter with that work necessities clarification both of the manner in which his practice makes such demands and also with the way these conceptual repositionings are themselves to be understood. One does not precede the other. They work together.

Painting continues. What counts however is way that continuity is understood. Were it to be mere continuity then painting would have been given an idealized presence as though it were either the 'idea' of painting that was being continued, or that form had become the expression or revelation of that which had a quality that was different from the work's material presence. Escaping from the hold of idealism can only occur by insisting on the materiality of art work. That insistence brings with it its own history. Production, once understood as a series of techniques, has a history. Painting continues with the recognition that it takes place after photography. While the 'after' could have been simply ignored, there are paintings—art works—for which the 'after' provided the point of departure. If the digital has replaced the photographic (replaced it by incorporating it) then this marks an interruption within the history of the image. More significantly, it is one that continues to register within painting. Henceforth, painting occurs in the era of 'digital reproducibility'. This is of course a general claim that allows for the interpretation of certain forms of contemporary practice as well as providing the means to allow for another repetition—repetition as a form of productive reworking—of art's history. What is opened at the same time is the way to Hawley's work.

2.

Hawley's work has long concerned the relationship between forms of visual repetition and question of production. Works that seemed to be patterns that had been interrupted to allow for framing—framing being no more than the work acquiring singularity—were juxtaposed with others that while evincing similar production techniques relied on a visual force other than patterning. This strategic use of the diptych characterized the body of work produced in 2004 under the general title *Zoom*. The series of works produced in 2006, *Timing*, introduced a further complication into the process. While the techniques had a similar register, they incorporated disruption and manipulation into the process.

Interrupting the technical—an interruption integral to production—did not demand the presence of the calculating hand of the artist. On the contrary, it became a way of linking production to chance.

Hawley's most recent body of work: *Something Else*, brings important new elements into a continually developing project. These introductions however are not mere additions. They have a two interrelated components. In the first instance they need to be understood as new engagements with the relation between production and materiality. The second element is that in this body of work there is a continual refinement of the individual works' relation to the history of painting. In regard to the second, though these two elements are from the start connected, that relation is not staged in terms of either symbolism or the layout of the work itself as though there were an internal diagram deployed within specific paintings. The connection in Hawley's work is evident in the way the works engage the wall. If it is true that sculpture eschews the planar then while the latter receives its affirmation within painting, the planar has more than one formal determination. In this series, the engagement with the wall is one of the central ways in which the components defining the works are related.

Rather than each individual work being presented on flat wood boards as occurred in earlier projects the paintings now appear on thick transparent plastic. (This material's transparency is central to the project of *Something Else*.) As a consequence, the flatness that was taken to define the project of modernist abstract painting is distanced. However, this is not the result of the addition of figures recalling and allowing for the possible introduction of perspectival space into abstraction. The distancing occurs because the surface now has a radically different quality. While they cannot be distanced absolutely there are three aspects of these works that begin to define the singularity of the overall project. The first concerns their relation to the wall. The second is the process of production and the third comprises the curatorial demands made by the works as a whole.

Prior to taking them up it is important to note in advance what these aspects identify. In each instance they locate work. They allow for the incorporation of titles and the placing of work within both a literal as well as a historical context. The three do not just provide the constitutive elements of the work. Rather, they delimit the way matter and production are combined. The combination comes to figure within writing once writing becomes criticism. The latter's concern is with the question of the way a work works as art. The continual attempt to respond to this question is the undertaking of a philosophically informed criticism. Even if there cannot be a definitive answer to that question, criticism takes art's material presence as the site of work. Its point of departure is the work of matter. Meaning is always an after effect of that work. If there is a way of capturing that material presence as 'at work'—a work that is always a staging and a presenting—then it is in terms of mattering: i.e. matter and materiality as activities.

3.

The first aspect noted above that needs to be taken up concerns the relationship between the works and the wall. In this instance the works' material presence cannot be readily assimilated to a setting in which art positions the wall as a neutral element in its own self-presentation. With this project—*Something Else*—transparency coupled to the actual or potential curl of the plastic taken in conjunction with the use of metal clasps to secure the works to the wall combine to give the wall a presence that can no longer be equated with a ground whose relation to art work could then be described in terms of indifference. In addition, the wall also emerges through the transparent plastic. This occurs because the application of paint is no longer co-terminous with the support. It is not as though there has been the creation of blank spaces. Rather, the showing of the wall through the plastic establishes what can be called spaces of neutrality within the work itself. Here examples are pertinent as they make mattering specific.

In *Constellation* these zones are both internal to the field of paint as well as marking the limit of that field. In regard to the latter while there is a point at which the literal application of paint ends, the transparency of the plastic allows the work of painting to continue. What is maintained is painting's engagement with colour and therefore more generally with presentation. The work operates as much through its projection of the internal as it does through the presence of the external internally. Within the painted field the incorporation of the wall is always there within (and as) zones of neutrality. The difference is that the wall intersects with the layers of paint. Varying forms of depth are present. However, they are forms in which there is the continual interplay of the literal layers of paint with the zones of neutrality. The literality in question involves modes of repetition allowing for the presentation of a patterning that recalls the work's engagement with the technical.

While the second aspect to be taken up pertains to the process of the works' production and therefore is an engagement with the technical, what is central is the content of the actual presentation. The works *Accumulation, Irregularity* and *Streaking* contain interrelated elements. The combination of layered paint in different colours—the mode of combination is again integral to the process of creation—is coupled to the way the repetitive pattering is interrupted from within, as though the work has to stage and incorporate a form of internal divergence. When taken together they work to produce a blur. (Blurring takes place in a number of works.) While these individual aspects may demand consideration in their own right, the blur provides a point of departure. The blur gestures in at least two directions. Firstly, it stages a relation to painting's engagement with photography and other forms of technical reproduction. This sense of the blur however stages the question of sequence. Is the blur an 'after effect'? This is clear as much from Gerhard Richter's paintings of photographs which are then presented as blurred as it is from his blurred abstract paintings. The question of the blur as 'after effect' in which the process of production invariably intersects with the philosophical problem of representation. In the case of Hawley's work the blur resists the question of sequence as it is both the result of the way the paint is layered (layering and colouring working together) and equally because it results from the interruption and continuity of repetition. Serial continuity incorporating its own form of interruption—as already indicated, divergence as interruption—inscribes the blur both within the work and beyond the hold of the elementary structures of representation.

The other direction to which the blur gestures is more literal. The blur is inherently visual. The blur is seen by a body positioned in front of the work. Painting's relation to its own visuality is more often noted than taken up. While perspective organizes the visual field, these works which involve the interplay of the layering of paint and zones of neutrality, resist any incorporation of perspectival space. Part of their mattering is blurring. The blur however is the moment at which the body's relation to the work is no longer circumscribed by spatial organization but by the continuity of the work's projection into space. Precisely because it is the continuity of that projection that is integral to the work's work, time takes precedence over the work's internal spatial organization. Time, in this instance, is fundamental to mattering. Moreover, it is time that defines the relationship between the blur and the body.

The third aspect pertains to the curatorial imperatives that arise once mattering begins to define work. Unlike other works that make up this project, and which then have a direct relation to the wall, *Spiralling* has a mediated presence. The transparency of the plastic is itself laid over a coloured background. The colour shows through the work whilst becoming part of it. There is a complex procedure of layering at work here. In a sense this work announces what all the other works already know. The presence of the wall within the work, the interplay between wall and the painting's actual material presence, which becomes less determinate at the edge, means that the installation of these works forms part of the process of their creation as art. This is not the usual argument concerning the centrality of the curator. The argument has to do with their specific material presence. The curatorial project would no longer concern the position of works on the wall but would have to incorporate the different ways in which the wall was itself incorporated within the works. Precisely because there is a necessity to incorporate these demands into any account of the object—they are not contingent aspects of the work—the specificity of the work, its own mattering, continues to make demands on curatorial strategies. Those demands once taken in conjunction with the other aspects that begin to define this body of work also yield exigencies for the project of writing.

While these elements mark out Hawley's work they open a space in which it becomes possible to define the ways in which art matters. Art's mattering, however, is not singular. Matter as the precondition for meaning creates the setting in which a confrontation with art and thus the dissesenus that art necessitates, needs to be understood as a result of work. Meaning on its own can never be the pure space in which art is present. Art presents itself through its mattering. Arts matters.

TRACES OF ANONYMITY

Art will always continue to exert a hold. However, that hold—a fixing in which the eye is encountered and thus within which the work becomes what it is—cannot be effectively separated from the means creating the image. Videos, video images that become photographs, paintings that acknowledge and affirm their relation to their own digital inception, define some of the means for image creation within the work of Jess MacNeil. And yet, what is at work within this particular project is as much indebted to the history of the image as it is to the mark of art's continual reworking of its own means of production. (A reworking that is part of transformation of the art object.) MacNeil's extraordinary *Opera House Steps* is a case in point. The work is present as a video, as a potential video still and then is repositioned within paintings. Prior to any comment on this work it is essential to recognize that what it recalls—an act of recall within an almost irresistible inevitability—is Alexander Rodchenko's 1929 photograph 'Steps'. Rodchenko's image of a woman holding a child while carrying a shopping basket and walking up stars (public stairs) inscribes the human subject as central. The medium allowed for little else. Nonetheless, her presence cannot be reduced to the sentimental humanism that marks depiction within both painting and photography. The captured moment stages the complex interplay between anonymity and public presence that marks contemporary urban life and which photography continues to enact. This is a setting in which it is essential to locate MacNeil's *Opera House Steps*. The video holds these steps in place. Movement is the passing shadows. Their presence, the shadows playing over the already fixed steps, does not represent absent figures. Rather than the movement of the shadows which demand that the steps as the location of the public are held in place, there is the continual creation and recreation of what can be described as *particularized anonymity.* The difference is fundamental. As the paintings emerge from the video—the video having become a static image which in turn has become the site of painting—not only is there the obvious connection between different genres of image there is a more profound recognition concerning the relationship between abstraction and anonymity.[18]

Once abstraction is moved beyond its simple and simplistic identification with the negation of figure, it can be redefined as much in relation to the history of abstraction as to the presence of anonymity. Questions that seek to establish meaning or identity can begin with an original site that is neither confused nor ambiguous. The prompt for such a question would be the anonymous. The problem of identity within a prevailing sense of both anonymity and dislocation is a continual refrain within modernity. The public as a location does not answer such questions it merely relocates them within that further definition of modern subjectivity in which being-in-place can be identified with the urban. What differentiates MacNeil's investigation and presentation of this condition from Rodchenko's can be located in the effect of different forms of image creation. It is not just MacNeil's video, and the editing techniques it allows, that are important, the inscription of the continuity within the loop creates the effect of a continuity of passage. As the shadows move the question—Who moves?—has an insistent quality. The 'who' will always be the potentially particular within the anonymous. Such questions are internal to the effect of the image. In the case of Rodchenko's gelantin-silver print any concern with the next step—her next step and thus question of who she may be—takes place beyond the image. That such questions are always external in the sense that they demand that the image continue is an effect of the way the image is created. Moreover, abstracting from her presence necessitates effacing the image. MacNeil's image is already an abstraction as it is from the start the presentation of the anonymity, always particularized, of place.

Particularized anonymity is concerned with traces and thus with the interplay of continuity and discontinuity. The traces,

18. I have taken up the relationship between abstraction and anonymity in my 'On Abstraction: Notes on Mondrian and Hegel', in Michael Asgaard Andersen and Henrik Oxvig (eds.), *Paradoxes of Appearing: Essays on Art, Architecture and Philosophy*, Baden, Lars Müller Publishers, 2009.

however, are only there as moments that are absorbed or which vanish. Within the medium of video there is the possibility to dwell of the continuity of tracing; a continuity that is defined by the inherent presence of the discontinuous. Of significance, however, is the twofold dimension that tracing involves. Marks, present as both modifying and disappearing, are only one aspect. The other pertains to that which is being traced. In the case of the *Opera House Steps* the trace of an anonymous other—anonymous while always particular—endures. As the video loops the inseparability of place and movement is enacted continually. Other recent video works by MacNeil are also concerned with this form of inseparability. However, rather than inscribe the mark of an anonymous other—there in the fleeting shadows of *Opera House Steps*—in the works *Wake (Coniston Water)* and *Wake (Windermere)* the complex process of passage itself is being staged.

These works both involve a split screen presentation of movement across water. 'Water' named and identified in advance. The movement leaves its mark while the water is itself marked. The latter form of marking involves, in the first instance, water's capacity to reflect. In addition, water is already the registration of wind, currents, etc. (Water *is*, in part, this registration. What are registered are not there as additions.) In other words, the inherent stability of a body of water is marked by its inherent instability. Both pertain. Hence there is a reiteration of the interplay of continuity and discontinuity. What allows for that interplay to be presented in this instance—and the instance is that which defines the image's specificity—is the relationship between water understood as a complex surface that is videoed and the presentation of that surface by two differentiated yet related screens. The screens present the water at different speeds and having a quality that differs. What differs is, of course, the same. What is the same, however, is that which can never be the same as itself namely water as a complex surface. Indeed, it is possible to go further and argue that the truth of water as a surface can only ever be staged within a set up that in refusing the literal—namely in refusing what is always thought to be the province of the photographic image—the truth of water, perhaps another 'literal' truth, can be staged. While it cannot be taken up here it is worth reflecting on art's struggles to capture and present the truth of water. Not to represent water but to present it as the site of that which is always working. Even still water is never still since it reflects.

There is a further aspect of both these video works that needs to be noted. What matters in both is the presence of a surface as that which stages. This is not to suggest that the surface can be thought independently of the process of staging. Rather what is revealed is that which opens up the connection between these video works and the practice of painting. Not painting *tout court* but the practice that MacNeil has been developing.) From the early series *Tenuous Ground* (2003) until the more recent *Videographic Paintings* (2007) MacNeil's concern is with what to paint. Part of the answer can be found in the way the digital or photographic image can be reworked to create the scene of and for painting. As such the surface no longer refers back to a setting there prior to its own creation. Nor, moreover, is the painted—the object encountering the eye—the site of a simple registration. The surface has become a palimpsest of images that while being one cannot be attributed a singular presence. If the water within *Wake (Coniston Water)* and *Wake (Windermere)* can only attain its truth through the refusal of literal presence, then the way the paintings appear to fragment, the way line and colour interplay with figure rather than being the means for its creation, provide a complex surface that enacts a similar refusal. The complexity in question is that which is proper to presentation. What is presented, not represented but presented as such, are the elements that only cohere within a setting in which coherence is the interplay of continuity and discontinuity. The figures and places with her work are neither individuals nor universals. They resist despair and utopianism. They demand a specific response. Her creation of images, a creation that cannot be thought outside the relation of the image to the digital, is the presentation of differing modes of *particularized anonymity*. As such she has become a presenter of modern life.

THE WORK OF FIGURES
Notes on the Art of Peter Neilson

If there were a definite perhaps defiant gesture made in the direction of photography—a gesture on behalf of painting occurring in the early years of photography's registration—then it is the unresolved left hand in Manet's 1878 *Self-Portrait*. Painting is not simply affirmed through the presence of palette and brush, the hand's presentation, taken in conjunction with the rest of his body, could only have ever been the work of painting. And yet, this affirmation, while real, harbours a more complex and dramatic development that is at work in a number of Manet's most significant paintings.

The supposition concerning this other development is straightforward. In part, it is there both in response to the presence of photography and to developments within painting. The claim is that central works by Manet can be understood in terms of the use of figure to trouble and remake the space of the figure within painting. (A remaking in which a singular space becomes the plurality of spaces.)

If the space created by perspective is the space created for and by the subject, and then even though that space will be undone by the process in which the art of the early twentieth century will become abstract, it is also the case that figures can have a similar effect. In other words, figure breaks its relation to the singularity of the subject by undoing, through its mode of presentation, the actual space of the figure. There is therefore a resulting transformation of the figure. Moreover, other forms of figuration are allowed as a consequence. What this means is that once the hold of perspective on the subject, a hold in which the subject is only possible because of perspective—a hold in which subject and figure are conflated—is no longer in strict control then there is a resultant undoing of the singularity of the subject positions inside the frame and the singularity of the one outside. (Both of these settings are given by the unanimity of position demanded by the singularity of perspective.) There is only one position from which to see. What is seen is given by the position created for the subject that is then seen. To the extent that the figure is retained, the undoing of the expectation of the relationship between subject and perception is the remaking of the figure.

While this position can be argued for in relation to many of Manet's works, a clear instance of what is involved is evident in *Mlle V ... in the Costume of an Espada* (1862). There are three groupings that involve the figure. There is Mlle V herself. She is turned towards the viewer: looking out whilst looking past the viewing subject. A matador on a horse in the process of spearing a bull is between Mlle V and a group of individuals standing by a back wall. There are other figures within the frame. While the frame contains depth insofar as there is the interplay of light and dark within the frame (included in the latter are cast shadows) the figures are not held within that depth. In other words, the figures have a disjunctive relation with the singularity of the figure that would be demanded by the relationship between narrative and presence provided by the work of perspective. At work here are different economies. One cannot be reduced to the other. Coherence is defined in terms of this original event of plurality.

What has been identified as 'undoing' needs to be understood as eschewing the nihilism of simple destruction in favour of remaking: destruction as creation, though equally created works as forms of destruction. However, the way Manet opens the frame to other modes of figuration should not be understood in terms of a mere proliferation of possibilities for the figure. That opening is the move from a form of singularity—the interplay of perspective and depth—to the incorporation of a complex plurality in which figures will figure henceforth. What this means is that while perspective will be retained, though only in terms of its incorporation within a plurality of sites, the frame will contain differing forms of figuration; each moment bringing with it its own operative sense of perspective and depth. Each one has therefore its own economy. In lieu of the singularity of relation that the tradition of perspective demands there will be a complex of relations without synthesis. As such, what is distanced continually is the possible identification of the site of painting's work in terms of the singularity of perspective and depth. It is as though the possibility that is there in Manet's *Mlle V ... in the Costume of an Espada* is taken to the extreme; i.e. a repositioning in which each element is allowed a space of its own. Singular spaces overlap or double: recreating the place of painting as a palimpsest of possibilities.

This recreation of a complex plurality provides the position in which to locate the work of figures in the paintings of Peter Neilson. Narrative in painting cannot work other than in relation to the operation of perspective. In Neilson's recent work there are a significant number of narrative paintings. What, however, do they narrate? Narrative in literature cannot be divorced from modes of temporal sequence. Narrative is always timed. The same is true in painting. In the case of classical perspective, in most instances, the eye is drawn into a focal point and then moves to incorporate other elements that comprise the structured and intended unified order that is depicted. In the case of singular perspective, narrative and time work together to reinforce the work's overall sense of singularity. Within the unfolding of the singular a unified structure can be seen. Neilson's narrative paintings work otherwise. The sense of alterity that these different works introduce lies within the impossibility of unity. The eye cannot hold the work together because there are openings, perspectives, folds of representation, different frame of activity, all of which work together to create and sustain the work.

Neilson's individual narrative paintings frame and reframe their complex content. Mirrors contain images that are projected back to the viewer who then must incorporate this distancing within the frame as forming part of a series of framed moments. The moments are not part of a synthetic whole. The works keep opening up different spaces. Each one is consistent. The spaces overlap. One opens onto and then within another. The overlapping in question, however, is not the overlapping of the same, it is the encounter of spaces in which differences can only be explained in terms of the creation of different relations within the frame. The literal frame therefore exerts both an arbitrary yet necessary hold. Spaces and framing devices work with and through figures. In *Through Dreams, Seen* there is an inside and outside within the literal frame. Part of what is framed includes a floor that opens and which in opening reveals another world in which figures are present. That opening is itself framed and thus is as much present as a frame as it is an opening in a floor. Each space has an indeterminate quality. And yet it has an actual quality. What is actual, however, is at the very least a doubled presence. In the top right hand of this painting a female figures gazes into a mirror. Mirrors play a significant role in Neilson's work. Mirrors, and thus the work of reflection, already figure within the history of painting. If they can be attributed a generalized status then it can be argued that the mirror is that which evokes both the ease and the immediacy of reflection. As such the mirror becomes the inscribed presence within painting of painting's attempt to project a unified whole. *As in the mirror, so in the painting* would become the rubric accounting for the presence of the mirror. The envisaged relation would reinforce the sense of expectation that was already there within the work of perspective. It would be as though the relation between the mirror and the one viewing literally mirrored the relation between the viewer (the subject) and the painting itself. Immediacy and unity would be the elements whose presence structured the relationship between the viewer and the viewed. That relation structures the subject positions.

This is the setting in which the mirror in *Mirror Mirror on the World* as well as mirrors in other works needs to be understood. That mirror is only ever the opening of a specific site. It is the staging of a mode of reflection that neither determines other sites of viewing—thus they are not present in terms of either ease or immediacy—nor provides the structure of viewer/viewed (subject/object) relation. Where those relations are taken to pertain for the entire work. However, there is more at work here than a distancing of certain modes of reflection and thus of immediacy. If works such as *Mirror Mirror on the World* can be understood in terms of the co-presence of differing sites, each structured by shifting loci each with their own sense of depth, then the works become an opening up and thus an allowing. 'Allowing' needs to be understood formally. To allow is not to create a particular already determined event. It is not to determine in advance the quality of an event. To allow involves the creation of a space. Rather than art having as its constraint the depiction of an event, to position 'allowing' in the place of depiction necessitates not simply the creation of places of activity but occasions and thus to present activity's inherent and ineliminable complexity. This is not perspectivism, as though there were just different views of the same and singular phenomenon. On the contrary, allowing for the event—an allowing structured by the abeyance of the singularity of perspective—is to open up the possibility of differing figures interacting within and through a range of spaces. The event is originally plural. These spaces are only held together. Once this condition is taken to be the order of things Neilson's work becomes a form of realism.

In the painting *The Two Way Mirror (Cinderella as Spy)* while Cinderella chats over a bar, another women stands with one leg within a frame. She has either backed into the frame, or she is stepping from it. The frame, however, is not a mere frame. It is clearly a photograph. Within the frame there are other photographic images. Tracing a line from the bottom left of the frame there is a movement across photographs that are present within an open draw. Photographs that were hidden have been revealed as the draw opened. On the desk is another photographic frame from which a man walks. Not simply has another space been opened the radical shift in scale is now involved in the creation of another space within the overall frame. Propped against the bar at which Cinderella sits is another photograph. Its size is discontinuous, of necessity, with other modes of photographic presence. That latter photograph is the one from which the woman walks (or backs into). Here is the production of a complex event; a pluralized site of possibilities. Scale, differing yet interacting framing devices, forms of layering, etc. working to allow the organizational logic of a range of works. Indeed the detail of works such as *Strangers in Our House, Thought Dreams* and *Mythmaking: Vile Gossip* amongst others would need to be taken up in these terms.

Having reworked the figure, the figure held within modernity in a position that recalls both the portrait and the cartoon, that figure is now able to gesture, to evoke, to stage in ways that open. Those openings have as their point of departure a severance between figure and character. Character had set the measure in relation to which the individual figure was to be judged. The interplay of character and figure was dependent upon an enforced singularity that was given as much by the work of perspective as it was by an overriding sense of decorum. Both are recalled though in their abeyance. As a result individual works such as *Clown, The Scoundrel, Hero Journalist* etc. become ways of presenting that take the reworking of the figure as their condition of possibility. No longer held by already given senses of propriety the figure is able to work again. The figure brings with it therefore another set of questions and thus demands different modes of evaluation. It is thus possible to return. *Mythmaking: Vile Gossip* inscribes a viewer. A figure within the frame looks at a setting that is already doubled. Each component of that doubling is itself a site working with its own sense of depth and thus its own perspectival demands. With the frame—framed—she stands and she looks. What does she see? What is she allowed to see? The answer is clear. What is allowed is the work of figures and thus the play of an insistent more than one: in sum, work as the plural event.

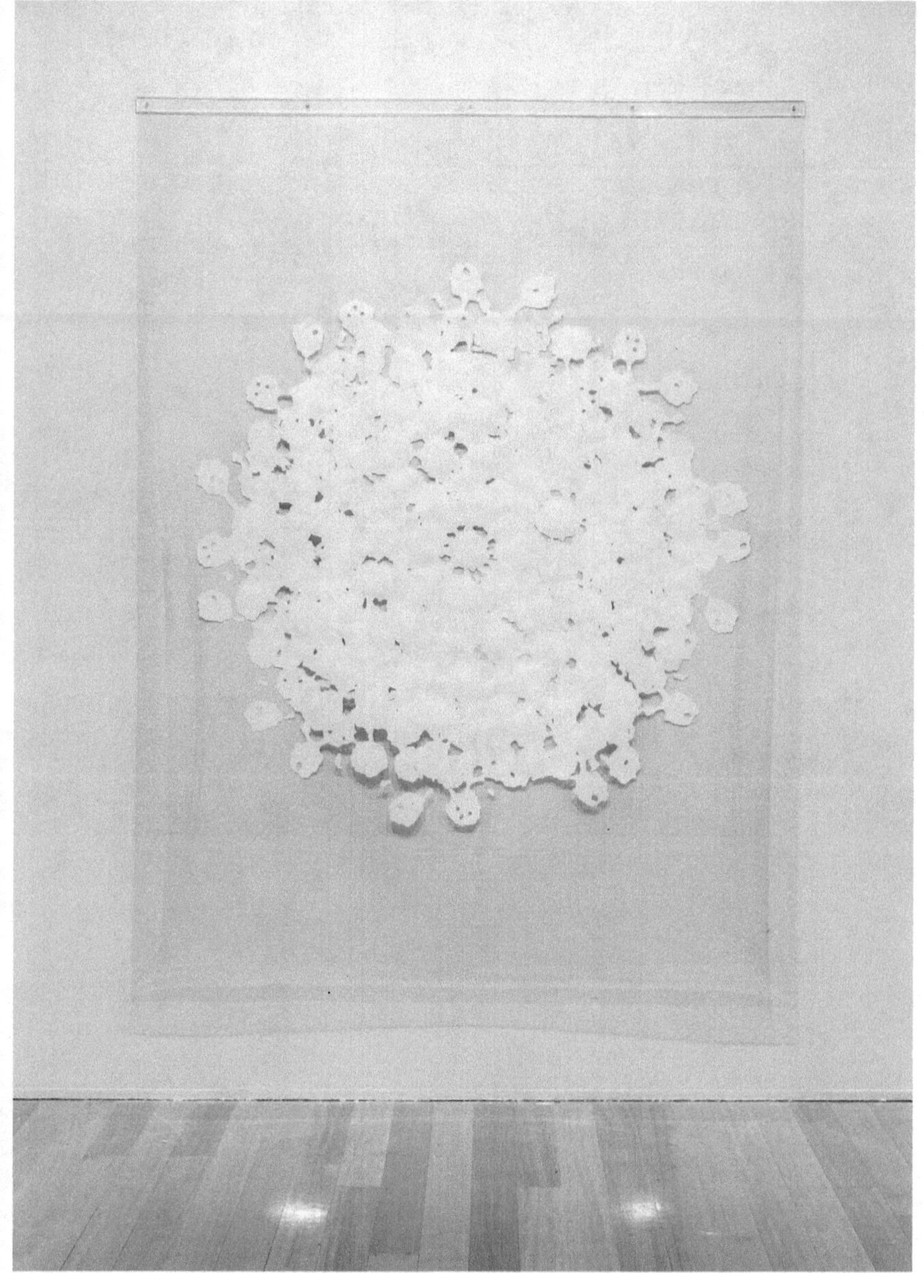

26. David Hawley, *Accumulation*, Screen-print on UV-resistant PVC, 225 x 180 cm, 2007.

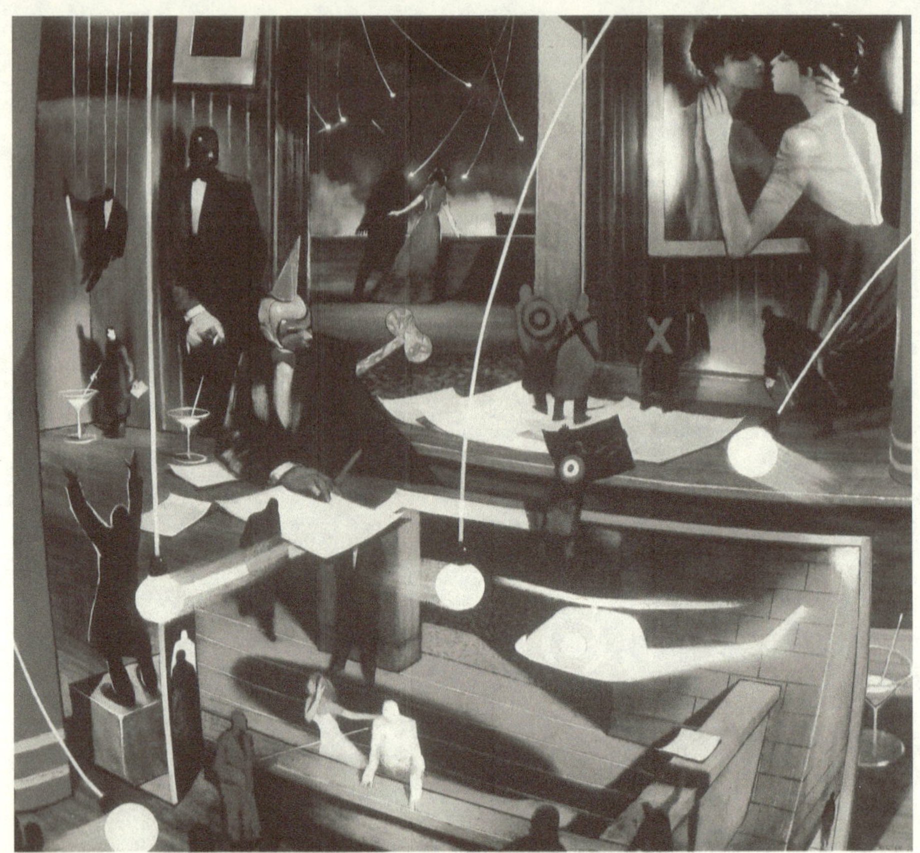

27. Peter Neilson, *Mirror, mirror on the world (seven random targets)*, oil on linen, 100 x 100 cm, 2008.

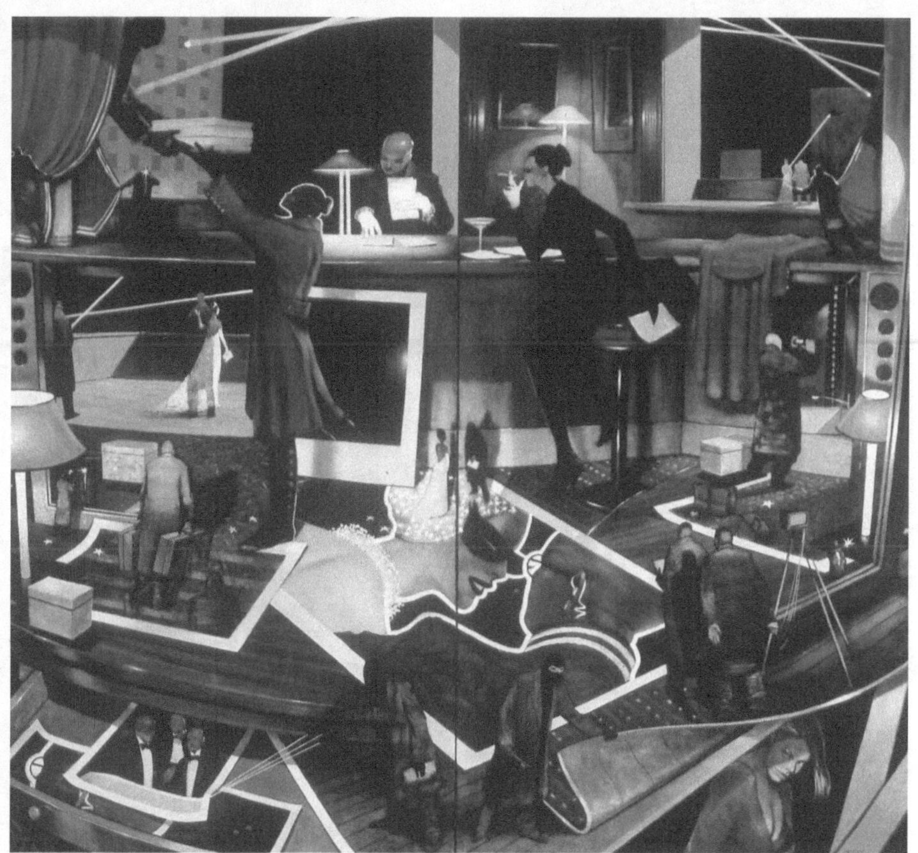

28. Peter Neilson, *Title, The two-way mirror: Cinderella as spy (never suspected, she lived happily ever after the overthrow of the Prince's brutal junta)*, oil on linen, 185 x 200 cm (two panels), 2007.

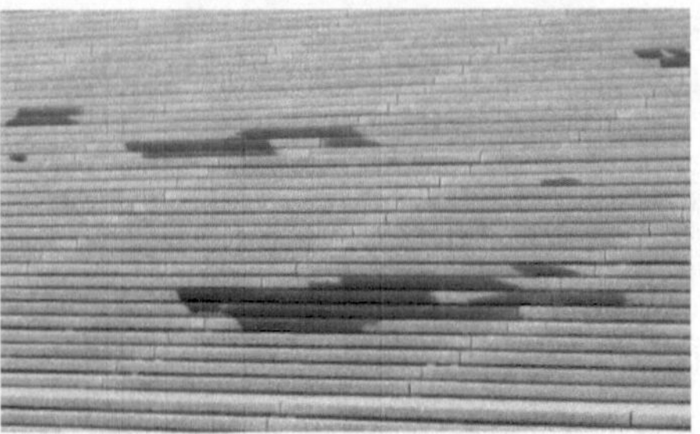
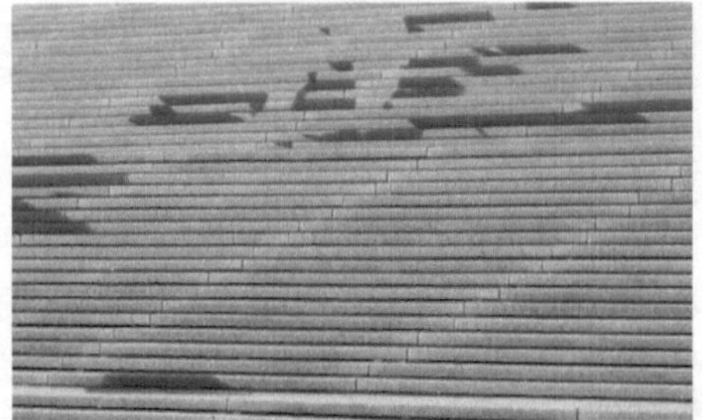

29. Jess MacNeil, *Opera House Steps: December*, digital video with sound, 2 min. 22 sec. infinite loop, 2006.

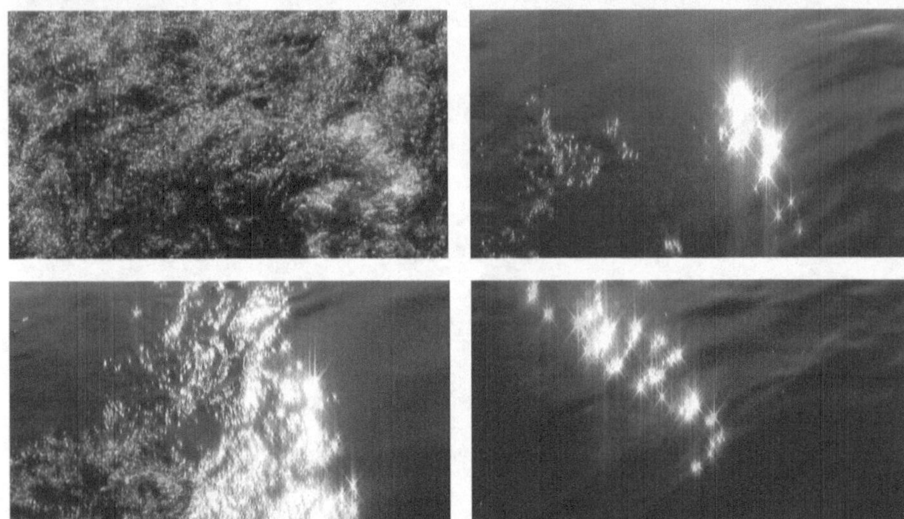

30. Jess MacNeil, *Wake: Coniston water*, dual channel digital video, 15 minutes 16 seconds, 2007.

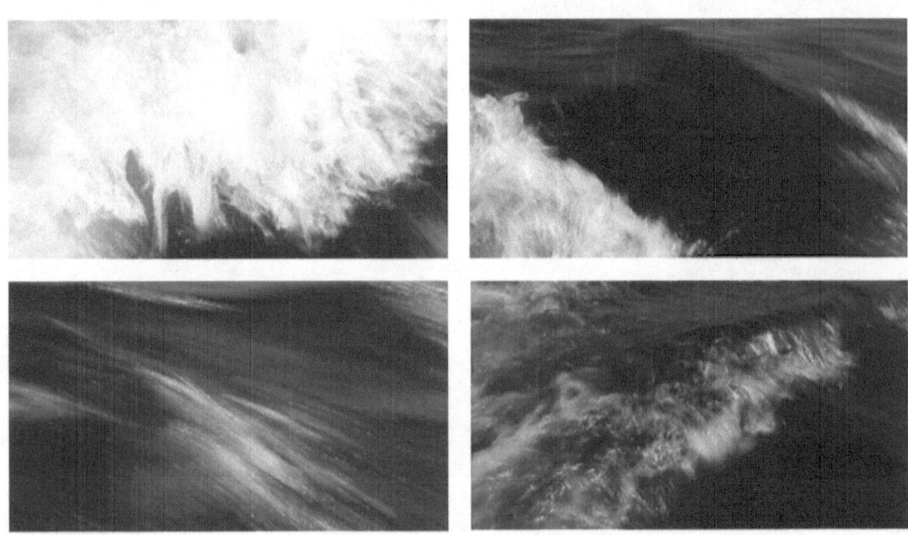

31. Jess MacNeil, *Wake: Windermere*, dual channel digital video, 13 minutes 43 seconds., 2009.

SCULPTURE

VANDALIZING OBJECTS, DESTROYING ART
Notes on Terri Bird's Recycling Fictions of Being

The destruction of a work of art, whether complete or partial, is part of the risk that art always brings with it. The vandalization of Terri Bird's recently installed sculpture *Recycling Fictions of Being*, which had been sited in the Alistair Knox Park in Eltham, makes its documentation an urgent concern.[19] Equally, however it allows for reflection to be given to art's almost necessary relation to iconoclasm. There is almost something remarkable about the capacity of humans to create objects or images, ones that are not instrumental in any direct sense, and yet which invite the destruction unleashed by vandals, fundamentalists, censors, etc. There are, perhaps, certain images, even art objects, whose destruction could be defended. And yet, even that defence would have to concede that what was being repeated is the iconoclasm that accompanies the history of the creation of images and works of art. Here, iconoclasm has a more contemporary feel. It can no longer be separated from the problem of the object.

Terri Bird's sculpture was situated in a suburban park. The important aspect of the location was that the work was placed on path created by pedestrians and walkers. The park itself is bounded by a street and the Diamond Creek. The created path functions as a short cut between the street and the creek, or the official path next to the creek. It generates an 'unofficial' line which Bird describes as 'a desire line'. The location of her sculpture to the side of this line, plus the nature of its presence—the latter being no more than how it worked as art—built upon and reinforced this

19. The work was commissioned by the Nillumbik Shire Council who biannually award the Nillumbik Art in Public Places Award. The Award was given in 2002. Her work was installed in March 2003 and destroyed by fire 8 weeks later.

unofficial positioning. And yet, the conventions of public art exist in relation to the official. Either a work commemorates and therefore its task is direct, or it complements an established terrain. Once a work complements what is given, then it can be justified as decorative. Such works can be defended because they have an inherently ornamental status. The ornament however is always attached. The site or place where they are assumed to belong, usually form part of an overall masterplan. It is the presence of this plan that defines the public. What this means is, of course, that whatever is intended by the term *public art* needs a conception of the public that is sufficiently complex to allow for a distinction between the official and the unofficial. There will be inevitable overlaps, a fact that locates, almost literally, the activity of graffiti artists.

The art of commemoration—of a monumentality that is always thought to be justified in advance—depends upon the effective and regulated presence of official public space. Bird's sculpture had an unofficial site. Its presence was the result of a negotiation with this conception of site. Works retaining the imprimatur of the official have difficulty referring to a site. They stand within it. The eschewing of monumentality, refusing a work evincing commemoration, means that a relation to site has to be more than simple location. Site needs to have a generative quality. This is clear with *Recycling Fictions of Being*. The nature of the relationship to site had a determining effect on the presence of her work. Given that it was a work of sculpture that presence had to do with its spatiality. Rather than address the site in terms of appearance, the sculpture was developed as a result of measuring the contours. The inflection of the contours—in positive terms and in terms of the generation of negative spaces—gave rise to a contour model. The model rather that simply mapping the site, took up its differing inflections. The geometry of the site was taken up in the work. The combination of the positive and the negative meant, that the actual work when finished gave the impression of both sitting on while also hovering over the ground. The question of relation—almost the brute physical question of the relation of the work to the ground—was there in the work's genesis and finally there in its completion.

The sculpture itself was constructed from recycled plastic panels. The recycling was not the repackaging that would be found in either the display of the *objet trouvé*, or the assemblages of Jessica Stockholder. Here, there is something different. The recycling involves an act of fabrication. Recycling in this context refers to the materials and not to their appearance. As the site is an artificial construct—the park and its contours have been created—since the 'desire line' is itself an addition, a fabrication after the event, then addressing the site means taking these elements into consideration as much as using the site's geometry as a generator.

The overall dimensions of the final object (300 x 1750 x 3650 mm), once taken in conjunction both with the way the work was positioned, and its relation to the ground, begins to account for its particular spatial presence. While always possible to describe such a project in negative terms, i.e. as the production of an anti-monument, this would be to miss the point. As a work it was not an anti-monument. Rather, and far more importantly, it was a work of public sculpture that could not be defined in terms of either monumentality or the decorative. (And this would be the case whether these terms were used to provide a positive description, or negative one such as the anti-monument.) What was important was twofold. In the first instance it was the nature of the relationship to site. Site was defined both by its geometry and its artificiality. (While not art, construing site in this way is to imbue it with quality of art.) The second was the way it complicated what is meant by term 'public', within the designation *public art*. This complication occurred because of the work's defining relation to the unofficial. In other words, its presence in the landscape, present as resting, touching, hovering, on and over the ground, raised the question of art in part because of its distancing the given conceptions of what art in the public realm is intended to do, and therefore what precisely the public is intended to be.

The language of paths and short cuts is bound up with questions of safety. Once stripped of any moral overtones then to wander from the path is to invite danger. Moreover, taking a short cut is to use a route devoid of propriety. Improper and dangerous behaviour invites destruction. Did the location of *Recycling Fictions of Being* in such a setting solicit vandalism? This is the perplexing question. Official art, in all its different guises, will always be the subject of a calculated response. Officialdom elicits it. The response therefore is as much to the art as it is to its symbolic content; a response that may have no relation at all to the particularity of the given work.

What happened here took place in relation to unofficial art. The argument therefore has to be that the destruction occurred because the work's presence as art was refused. Art becomes art when it is officially defined as art. A definition that is conferred as much by the market as it is by the art institutions. Once a work of art is sited outside that realm—as this one was—then it runs the risk of becoming an object. While it will always be true that art objects are objects, Duchamp's great invention was to dramatize this point, an additional element has been introduced. The risk art now takes—especially art that bears a difficult relation to the institutions—is for it to be destroyed, not as art, but as an object. Once this risk is recognized, moreover, once it is defined as a problem that arises because of the power of institutions—sites that are truly official—then the question of criticism is reopened. Given the inevitable presence of markets and institutions, accepting their power to delimit and define art, criticism will have to do more than debate such identifications. Beyond the hold of the official institutions, it can only be criticism that establishes the object's work as the work of art. There are no guarantees; in addition criticism will always be the locus of contestation. Nonetheless, once criticism takes on the task of securing the object's presence as art—then its destruction as an object becomes less likely. (It could, of course, still be destroyed as art.)

Only once a more nuanced sense of the public is developed will the risk of destruction begin to dissipate. It has to be a sense recognizing complexity, a recognition that was already there in the work *Recycling Fictions of Being*, part of its work as art. This possibility defines part of the task of contemporary criticism. Criticism cannot stem the literalization of the destructive impulse. It can however clarify its object.

SERRA AND THE SPACE OF SCULPTURE

Sculpture eschews the planar. In so doing, it becomes the site in which space and force begin to define each other. And yet, it is not as though this play of definition sustains an indifferent relation to site. What can be described as sculpture's mattering—namely, its material presence having an operative quality generative of meaning—allows sculpture to have a specific site. The latter is not a comment on either the museum or public space in any direct sense. Rather, it underscores the necessity that the space that sculpture creates is always within pregiven spaces. While painting can remain more or less indifferent to this sense of place, sculpture cannot. If there is a genuine relation between architecture and sculpture then it does not belong to a realm of resemblances or visible connection in which scale would be the only moment of distinction. The accord between them pertains to space making. While it is naïve to equate architecture with detail, it is equally as remiss to make the same equation with sculpture. Their accord, as well as the points of differentiation, are given by the way they maintain specific forms of space creation.

In sum, space creation discloses the point of connection. Equally, the different sense of the space created and the means by which it occurs closes it off. Sculpture 'matters' differently. The specificity of the interconnection between space, materials and the body defines the mattering of sculpture. The ways they are interconnected marks out the particularity of a given work.

Richard Serra's work which was on display at the Museum of Modern Art in New York in an exhibition that brings together forty years of projects is an important moment within the development of sculpture's capacity to create spaces.[20] Sculpture has

20. The exhibition took place June 3, 2007—September 24, 2007.

always produced spaces and as such implicates the body of the viewer in a manner that is fundamentally different to the way the body of the viewer regards painting or the way the body within architecture is situated. The inscription of the body, its having been positioned by work, is not just central to Serra's project; more significant is that the development of that project makes differing demands on the body.

More generally in regard to sculpture's material presence, it is difficult to separate force and space. If all sculpture creates space—space creation and bodily implication are related from the start—then there is an already present connection between the elements that delimit the mattering of sculpture. However, force needs to be given a more exact formulation. The relationship between a solid object and gravity is already a play of forces. While sculpture's attempt at monumentality simply assumes the positioning of the object, Serra's work, and this includes work from the 1960s as much as it does the most recent projects, operates in an importantly different way.

The series undertaken in 1969 and know as the 'prop pieces' explore the sense of tension that can inhere in a sculpture's presence. *One Ton Prop (House of Cards)* consists of slabs of lead that when placed together support each other. Rather than self-standing stability, weight and force are distributed within the work. Despite the solidity—a solidity reinforced by the natural colour of the lead and a scale that is almost equivalent to the body—the work seems tenuous. Tension and a form of fragility undermine any straightforward gesture towards the monumental. Other works in the series also exploit forms of instability that move the viewer away from any reverential approach to the work and towards the way that force and material are involved. It is as though the works' actual material presence only emerges as itself within the type of tenuousness that this particular form of mattering allows.

As Serra's work developed projects become larger in size. Scale however was not given by the perpendicular. Indeed with works such as *Intersection II* (1992-3) and *Torqued Ellipse IV* (1998) an importantly different relation to scale emerges. While the steel plates are tall—approaching 3 metres in height—what is significant is that they create spaces in which the viewer enters. The works tilt such that their quality of being inside or outside is importantly different. There is no uniform experience. The height allows the reality of the steel to impinge as it can become the object of direct focus. Equally, the effect of the volume on the body differs within the process of viewing. Material force has become affect. The viewer is continually positioned and repositioned insofar as both walking and resting are the two modes necessary to view these works. Indeed it is essential to note that while these works create space the experience of that space is defined by time. Experience is no longer delimited by the single view or the sedentary subject. Viewing involves moving and resting. Here is sculpture that demands process; time and movement marked by the interplay of sequence and pause.

The project set in motion by these works is continued by three later projects. *Sequence, Band* and *Torqued Torus Inversion* (2006). While it takes time to see them, they are importantly different. *Sequence* creates both internal an external spaces while *Band* involves a continuous encounter with an object that is over 20 metres in length. In both instances the body encounters that which should overpower it. However, the sensation that emerges is an acute awareness of the body's inherent spatial presence. Again, that awareness and thus the body's place in space are given through time. There can be no mastery of these objects and yet these works do not seek to master. They continue to stage encounters with work—a staging allowed by matter's creation of place—that can be as much idiosyncratic as collective.

With all of these works what cannot be forgotten is the Museum of Modern Art. The work of these sculptures occurs within a setting that seeks, in ways that are far from unproblematic, to define an encounter with the modern. What Serra's work opens up—and it is opened by the mattering of sculpture—is the question of the experience of art work. The question of that experience, and it is a question that should have genuine acuity precisely because it is often overlooked, concerns not just art's relation to the body but the role of the body in the viewing of art. As such Serra's exhibition makes demands that are internal to the exhibition itself, while at the same time allowing exhibition to emerge as an insistent question in its own right. This is the point at which sculpture touches the concerns of architecture.

FRAYING LINES
Richard Goodwin's City

> *What is at stake, if art is to truly infiltrate public space, is the skin of architecture.*
>
> Richard Goodwin.

OPENING

If there is a need to continue to return to the city as a site where the interplay of thought and activity, and forms of innovation are located, it is, in part, because subjectivity—and here it is tempting to add 'modern' subjectivity—knows nothing else. And yet, the relationship between city and subject cannot be explained in terms of cause and effect. As though affect were no more than an effect. Allowing subjectivity to emerge as a question—one that is always placed—requires the narrative of the city to move beyond mere description. While cinema and the novel may already know this, architectural configurations of the city often remain unmoved. What has to be allowed therefore is that place and the process of placing are locations of work. Being is, after all, an activity.

As the city is a site of movement in which interventions and adaptations undo the rigid distinctions defining modern urbanism, there is a corollary with the subject. The urban body is positioned and positions. With the body caught in flows that are defined by the relationship between movement and place, the conventions of an urbanism that works, not just in terms of defined oppositions (e.g. public/private, inside/outside, wall/pavement), but does so prescriptively are undone. (To which it should be added that this undoing locates the particular place of 'other' architectural projects. Hence the contention always has to be that the conventions of urbanism as generally practised, systematically fail to conceive of the locus of activity—the city—as a site that is inherently dynamic and affective.) As city spaces are taken over and positioned against the use envisioned for them; as market places occupy sites (though only ever on a temporary basis); as the ephemeral and the permanent work together, the borders and lines that define the city fray. Lines open. Spaces emerge.

Fraying within the city will work to re-define public and private spaces no longer as a binary opposition or as a matter of degree. The fraying of lines, the loosening of borders mark the implicit porosity of the urban.[21] There should, however, be no naïveté here. The fraying of city—its being rethought in terms of porosity—takes place under the silent though watchful eye of CCTV. Any attempt to think through the mapping of the city—the latter is a process that has an inherent plurality due to the differing possible prompts for such a project—must negotiate the presence of this eye. If, within the urban, 'I' see, there is, in addition, another eye that also continues to see. Physical sight will interact with a virtual one. Site and sight are imbricated. The presence of this other eye will in the end necessitate a link be established between fraying and forms of evasion. The continual overlapping of site and sight, while already a form of mapping dictated as much by questions of safety as a desire to control, must itself be subjected to its own form of fraying.

FOUR IMPLICATIONS

Neither given nor merely approached, the city as it figures within Richard Goodwin's projects, is a site in which 'other' projects become possible. An-other field is opened up. An urban terrain is positioned as a site of continual transformation. The principle and the process of transformation are internal to the site in question. Invention and intervention—their interconnection—occasioning

---

21. The term 'porosity' is central to Goodwin's own theorization of many of his projects. It is term he has used on a number of occasions to define the conception of the city at work in a number of his projects. Clearly what follows is indebted both to that theorization and its related practice. In addition Goodwin has run a continuous Design Studio on the theme of porosity at the College of Fine Art attached to the University of New South Wales from 2004. Equally, the use of 'porosity' is indebted to Walter Benjamin's text on Naples, one in which 'porosity' is the organizing motif. I have discussed Benjamin's Naples in detail in my 'Porosity at the Edge: Working Through Walter Benjamin's "Naples"', *Architectural Theory Review*, vol. 10, no. 1, 2005, pp. 33-44.

transformations occur within an already given place. They are not imagined as coming from without and projected onto a place yet to be named. Reconfiguring, as opposed to reform, operates by charging and changing the given. These considerations already indicate the theoretical dimension implicit in Goodwin's city projects. Central to them is that they depend upon the city of Sydney. And yet, the necessity inherent in the work's relation to Sydney has nothing to do with parochialism. The projects implicate Sydney. Theory and place double the sense of implication. Taken together they disclose—though only ever as a site of continual interconnection—four sites of implication.

No Longed for Utopia

In the first instance what is at work is a stance taken in relation to the preoccupation art and architecture have to the utopian. If a city project is utopian, then it posits another place. This positing cannot, as a consequence, have a transformative effect on the given. That would only occur, i.e. transformation is only possible, if the site in question is one in which the future projection, in being laced in, or threaded through the present, works to transform a site that is itself to be understood as inherently transformable. This creates the criteria for judging utopian responses to the city. To the extent that a project is radically differentiated from the present such that it is indifferent to the given, then what is problematic is not the presentation of the future within an already determined image. On the contrary, such a project is problematic because it positions the given as both static and thus unable to generate a place of radical transformation. Within the strictures of the utopian what cannot be allowed is a conception of the present that allows for its own transformation. The limit of utopian projections therefore—responses on the level of the image—resides in its conception of the given. Contrary to that which is implicit in the project of utopianism, the urban fabric is not static and is thus always open to interventions. Utopianism obviates the need to consider this as a possibility. (This state of affairs will re-emerge in terms of a relationship between Goodwin's projects and porosity.)

Sydney

Forced back to the particular, though not to particularity as opposed to universality but to the particular as the always determined demand of specificity, opens the way to Sydney. Sydney is therefore a particular instance. Recognizing Sydney's necessity, understood as the necessity to work though an already given site of transformation's continuity, means that a theory of the urban (once theory is understood, not as descriptive but allowing for the generative) necessitates a return to concepts such as the regional and the local. Rather than a generalized conception of place, what has to occur is the interplay of particularity and the identification of a given locality. What this means is that if there is an element in Goodwin's work that can be usefully abstracted—and useful abstraction can be defined as that which in opening up other sites, does so by allowing for the question of application to emerge as one that has to be resolved rather than as already positioned by a direct connection between the so-called 'pure and applied' let alone inhering in an already made image. This can only occur if those sites are also conceived as having been positioned by the relationship between the particular and the regional.

Modelling Cities

The third implication—allowing for the necessity of points interconnection—involves another path through the relationship between the urban and questions of transformation. The history of architecture contains forms of mapping that oscillate between simple descriptions and the creation of utopian visions. Not only does this occur on the level of mapping, it is also endures in collage and model making. From the incorporation of models of the City of God into paintings, to the creation of models that posit nothing less than the possible enactment of a secular utopian vision, models are an inextricable part of the utopian. While all of these instances bring with them important differences—and they are differences to which it is essential to be attentive—what each positions is a completed totality.

The completed future is always other. Even if every detail is not filled in what defines the vision/model is the intended radical differentiation from the city or urban configuration that is at hand. While it may seem that the counter position to the utopian vision of the city—a vision and accompanying image that may harbour the critical—is the acceptance of what is already at hand, this need not be the case. Were the present to be accepted—taken as the given with which urbanism is constrained to work, work and not transform—then such a position would stem from the premise that the given can never occasion its own transformation, or at the very least it would only allow for adaptation and development. What characterizes all such positions is that they are versions of an already present identification of the urban fabric with the complet(ed).

The instrumental relationship between the model and completion opens up at this precise point. (What is true of the model will also pertain to the drawing.) Completion emerges either as the image of the future that is given as complete and therefore the project, the move from model to construction, is to complete it. Or, it involves the acceptance of the given as already completed. To the extent that completion, in either sense, is distanced, then working with a specific site cannot have a predictable outcome. Drawing and models are part of a process in which an image is being worked out rather than having already been given. Such recognition should have an effect not just on planning but on the criteria of judgement that accompanies it.

In sum, Goodwin's projects are not to be understood as images of the future which, in virtue of this futurity, could be generalized and applied without any consideration being given to the place (and time) of their occurrence to other settings. They are 'workfull' interventions into a site—Sydney as an infinite plurality of sites—that is itself already a locus of continual transformation and therefore of potentiality. Openings emerge. They do so however, not because of projections—forcing the future onto the present—but through the process of fraying.

Fray

Wool and string fray when the tight line that they create begins to come undone. Within that line other spaces emerge. Material frays when its edges begin to open, allowing for the intrusion of differing elements. If the other possibility within this process can be deployed—a possibility in which fraying can be held back from the affray that it might become—then a fray not only introduces movement and dynamism thought as forms of excitement, it also gestures to the ineliminability of forms of conflict that are inherent in the urban. Precision is essential here. Conflict is not war. Fraying need not become the affray. Nonetheless, speed, power, subjectivity, etc. work within and through sites, constructing them as inherently differential and complex from the start. Fraying is an original condition.

The question of safety should not involve the homogenization of sites of fray. Rather, fraying as a condition needs to be made productive. There is an important critical dimension here. The intrusion of a wall that is intended to mark a complete division and thus an absolute separation—whether this be the green line across Nicosia in Cyprus or the wall attempting to divide Israel and Palestine—is one that in attempting to eliminate an affray, does so on the condition of continual policing. A continuity that invites affray as a possible, though perhaps in the long run as an inevitable, response. Allowing for fraying therefore does not result in the destruction of lines, or their passive acceptance. Fraying marks the introduction—an introduction building on an already present possibility—of complex spaces. Fraying undoes the hold of projected singular divisions.

These four implications—implications in the sense that they are already implied within Goodwin's projects, implicating the urban thereby implicating Sydney—create a point of departure. One that leads to the projects, though it is also one to which the projects lead. As a beginning therefore there is an already present reconceptualization of the city. The city is positioned henceforth as the site of movement and is thus able to incorporate other speeds and differing projects. As has already been indicated the nature of the incorporation depends upon particularity. Hence it matters that with Goodwin's work what is at play is Sydney, or at the very least a certain version of Sydney. Equally, transformations once understood as experimental and thus are not the imposition of an external other—the utopian fantasy—but involve the introduction of alterity into the given. What matters with this point of departure (and return) are the projects.

PROJECTS

a) Pyrmont and Cope Street Parasites

Prepositions define a sense of place. 'In', 'on', 'within', 'with' etc., all bring relations of place into consideration.[22] In addition, they

22. The aim here has been to link a number of different projects in order to identify a theme in Goodwin's work that involves porosity: the parasite and the exoskeleton. Having located them it becomes possible to approach them as much in these terms as it is by reference to fraying, transformation and original plurality. Goodwin's work forms an important part of an urbanism that maintains criticality while eschewing the utopian. (Where the latter is understood as the creation of of an already determined image.)

have aspects of inclusion and exclusion. What defines a number of them, within the urban, is a connection to a literal surface.[23] The surface may be an exterior wall. It could be an entrance foyer that divides and separates. It could be the ground 'outside' as opposed to 'inside' a building. The latter being a distinction re-enforced, thus maintained, by the exterior wall (also a surface). Were the surface no longer to be accepted as a dividing line, then not only would there be the need to employ a different set of prepositions—e.g. 'through' would have joined 'in' in order that a more complex set of spatial relations can be positioned—it would also be the case that the inherent stasis demanded by the initial configuration of the relationship between surface on the one hand and the opposition interior/exterior on the other hand would need to be reconsidered. The mediating presence of other prepositions indicates a different sense of spacing.

If a line is drawn through a site such that the interior/exterior and thus external and internal surfaces are only maintained within a system in which they lose their primacy, then fraying is at work. On a building in Pyrmont, running from the exterior of the building through the glass door and into the entrance foyer is a fifteen metre long steel sculpture (Pyrmont Parasite). Running from the inside to the outside and disregarding both the setting for an external sculptural presence and therefore fraying the absolutization of the distinction between inside and outside, the sculpture refuses the building's surface. The refusal becomes the process that the sculpture 'is'. The sculpture—now as a line—stages a form of fraying. Drawn through founding oppositions (e.g. inside/outside) it holds them in place. Nihilism is not a productive option in this context. However, it does so by eschewing the problematic of negation. Here there is another strategy. Alterity is produced and thus has the potential to be productive. That potential, however, does not lie in the possibility of the transference of the image. Rather, it inheres in the capacity to abstract the parasite's dynamic quality and thereby allow the question of what parasitism in another context—thus another place—would entail.

23. Here, I would want to insist on a distinction between literal surfaces and what I have called elsewhere the 'surface effect'. The latter defines a surface as that which delimits spatial enclosure. However, it is not automatically reducible to the literal surface. See Andrew Benjamin, 'Surface Effects: Borromini, Semper Loos', *Journal of Architecture*, vol. 11, no. 1, 2006.

The Parasite Façade in Cope St Alexandria draws elements of the Pyrmont Parasite into play while opening up a path leading to one of Goodwin's recent and most significant works, i.e. the Parasite Project at 345-363 George St. Even though a small scale project, what the Cope St Parasite Façade envisages is an architectural intervention that is not defined by the traditional logics of addition. The intervention, thus the project, will allow for an addition. And yet, what the parasite stages is an occurrence that is neither added on, thereby not repeating the original logic of construction, nor is it not present merely as a form of ornamentation.

Given that there is neither a traditional logic of addition nor one of ornamentation, the parasite works within while at the same time creating the space opened by the abeyance of these two modes of organization. The logic of addition necessitates that an extra element—the addition—is always determined by the organizational system to which it is added. There would need to be both a formal as well as a visual repetition. The question that arises in this context—the question situating Goodwin's project—concerns the possibility of an addition that is not determined by the organizational system of the original. To the extent that this is possible, there is a transformed conception of the original. Instead of the original having a quality that always dictates the presence of additions, it can be transformed by that act. Hence, the original becomes that which was itself transformable from the start. It is important to note that with this shift in how the original is understood the quality of the urban—the quality of its already being a site of transformation—defines the single building. In other words, the domestic is defined by the urban condition rather than in opposition to it.

The same question arises with ornamentation. In general, if there is a logic of ornamentation, then in functional terms it is indifferent to that which it ornaments. While such a position is more complex, for example when it concerns the use of colour in architecture, indifference pertains for the most part when functional considerations demand spatial presence. Ornamentation and adornment are inherently indifferent to function's spatial presence. While the work of these two logics—addition and ornamentation—will always need to be clarified further, what is evident in any of Goodwin's projects is not the negation of these logics, but their having come undone. Undoing is bound up with fraying. At Cope St there will be an addition. It will have ornamented and yet neither of these processes is explicable in terms of the logic in which they are traditionally situated. On the other side of nihilism, fraying creates.

In regards to the Cope St Parasite, what is initially undone is the external wall as that which defines and delimits space within the overall organization of the building. Again, ornamentation will not be defined by indifference. Within the project's own logic the external wall as a line is not broken. The parasite works through it. Living on it by contributing to it. Being positioned on it, the parasite works by repositioning what counts as the surface, the line is held and dispersed—frayed—such that while there is a form of repetition the system that produced the line no longer defines its presence. Its frayed presence is the result. Neither addition nor ornamentation, what could have mere refusal and thus destructive negation becomes *other.* The *other* in question is not the posited alterity of a discursive system but the presence of a spacing—a transformation of the given—occurring by having released the potential that was always there in the initial line. The link between transformation and potential is of central importance.

Lines cannot preclude fraying. What that means in this context is that the 'parasite'works on, in and through a system whose very structure and organizational logic is pitted against parasitism, and yet, its actual presence—straight lines, exterior wall, space conceived in terms of binary oppositions—cannot achieve this end.

b) Charles St Bridge / The Bond (Hickson Rd)

Even though they are importantly different Goodwin's Charles St Bridge and his sculptural intervention at The Bond (40 Hickson Rd Sydney) have an important affinity. If the former is architecture's relation to sculpture the latter reverses the position. At work in both however is a relationship between the work of passage and the work of the body. In both instances bodies move by traversing bridges and walking in and through an urban square. In regards to the latter it becomes urban, not by its literal presence in the city, but by a sculptural intervention one whose concerns with balance and spatiality, created through an interplay of materials as well as the levels and the differing height of the project's constituent parts, releases the urban's potential for transformation. Again there is the distancing of the logic of ornamentation. It is a distancing that is productive. It produces by transforming place as that which occasions. A space of encounter is disclosed. An opening in the city becomes public and thus other civic spaces emege in the process. One of the genuine strengths of Goodwin's projects is its insistence that public and private are neither given as a simple opposition nor is space public merely in virtue of its location. Space has the potential to become public. This works work by actualizing that potential.

Within the history of philosophy's engagement with architecture the bridge plays a central role. For Heidegger in 'Building, Dwelling, Thinking', the bridge becomes 'an example' of building.[24] Heidegger is uninterested in the bridge's material presence. His concern is with what it allows. As an object it 'initiates the lingering and hastening ways of men to and fro' (354). And yet, for Heidegger these are not mere 'men'. Rather they are 'mortals'. Those who stand before what he terms the 'divinities' and are positioned in relation to 'earth' and 'sky'. The bridge 'gathers' (355) all this together. Moreover, it allows them a 'site'. This combination—what Heidegger refers to as the 'four fold'—defines the original relation that human being has to place. The strength of Heidegger's position is that it rids the question of being human of any residual humanism by allowing whatever it is that is proper to being human to be always placed. However, the strength of Heidegger's position is also its weakness. If human beings encounter place, this does not occur under the heading of either 'men' or 'mortals'. It occurs in relation to originally complex modes of urban being.

While place is fundamental, the urban understood as a site of continual transformation in which movement and possibility are essential, unfolds in relation to embodied beings. Only by assuming the primordiality of embodiment does it then become possible to allow both for potentiality and transformation—on the level of subjectivity—to be the site of differences. These differences do not just play themselves out in relation to questions of race, ethnicity and gender; they also concern the abled and disabled bodies, the child's body, the ageing body, etc. Urban bodies are therefore never just one.

The complexity of the body or its opposite—the unity of human being demanding the body's excision—has its corollary with the bridge. (The compatibility of structure between the urban

24. In Martin Heidegger, *Basic Writings*, ed. and trans. by David Farrell Krell. Harper, San Francisco, 1993, pp. 343-365. Page references given in the body of text.

and the body—complexity on the one hand and Heidegger on the other—involves the differing ontological configurations within which they are positioned. Corollary is not analogy.) Given this setting, it matters that Heidegger will not discriminate between bridges. Each will play its part in regard to the relation between human being and place. What, however, if the bridge's material presence were to matter? Not just its materiality in terms of the relationship between suspension and passage as the work of materials, but the more demanding relation between materiality, functionality and affectivity.

Goodwin's Charles St Bridge demands attention. That demand occurs explicitly in relation to its presence as a bridge. The twist of bars that construct it hover at a point that allows sculpture and architecture a point of address. And yet, the project's power resides in its being a bridge. Moreover, the appearance of the bridge refuses the symmetry that defines traversal. Symmetry already evokes a form of affective neutrality. Here the form demands a different response. What has to be considered with this bridge is that its affective quality, and thus its presence as a bridge—bridge as opposed to sculpture—,cannot be separated from its particularity. Once the detail is given the attention it warrants then were it to become a bridge within the philosophical then it could not be assimilated to Heidegger's project. It is not just that its presence matters—in relation to which it should be noted that its material presence is its particularity—particularity and materiality in refusing both generality and the logic of exemplarity such that this bridge could, *qua* example, not be substituted for any other, becomes a repetition of the capacity of place to be transformed. If that is the case then the capacity for the original relation between human being and place is also reconfigured in the process.

The ground of transformation is the original plurality of place. In sum, that ground is a fraying that was already there. Hence a set-up whose potentiality can always be released. A possible occurrence that endures precisely because the line cannot eliminate the interplay of potentiality and fraying. Equally, therefore, on the level of affectivity and urban being the capacity for transformation—a position defined, once again, in terms of potentiality—assumed an original complexity in relation to human being. An ontology of original complexity is at work. (Neither place nor subjectivity are settled—let alone settled once and for all.) As such neither 'mortals' nor 'men' are involved in forms of traversal. Bridges have the capacity to allow for original sites of difference to be present. In this instance, matter makes such a demand.

c) 345-363 George St. Parasite

Rather than working through the opposition between the inside and the outside—working through it by fraying the line that held the division in place—the parasite in this instance begins to occupy spaces within buildings that allow for fraying as much as invention. Working its way through at least two existing buildings—a working through that attests to porosity as an original condition—and the streets and lane ways running between them, the parasite colonizes spaces and in so doing transforms them. Here is invention *post facto*. This project will deploy created walkways and thus manufactured architectural interventions as much as it will use the already manufactured (the ready made/found objects etc.) to create spaces. The combination of the two senses of manufacture brings together differing elements of Goodwin's work. The use and reworking of the ready-made recalls the sculptural and urban projects linked by the term 'Exoskeleton'. (A term central to Goodwin's own critical vocabulary.) The entry into pre-exiting buildings is a theme that has already been noted.

What is significant in this project is not just the projected scale—though scale cannot simply pass unnoticed—but the fact that as the parasite intrudes into the building, spaces that were hidden are opened up. Spaces that were private begin to take on a public quality. Layers and depths within existing spaces are either grouped or individuated. A new logic of construction operates with and against—and it is important to note that it is both—the prevailing ones. However, Goodwin is not offering a simple drawing project, as though the benign act of redrawing in order to discover what had not been noted before carried with it a potential to transform. Such projects often do no more than maintain existing lines and then draw through and around them. Discovery within such a practice remains oblivious to fraying's original potentiality and the possibility of its release. Goodwin's project will not be content with drawing. Nonetheless, with this project the parasite's materiality, its combination of the created and the found opens this project up beyond the confines of drawing and representation.

The parasite works through buildings. What were initially separated, are joined. The connected allow for forms of separation. This does not work on only one level. It carries up through the buildings. The parasite works its way up, through and across five floors. What is taking place can only be understood if it is positioned in relation to the assumption that the location of borders has already been established and the edges—e.g. the points of differentiation between buildings or between roads and buildings—are given. This parasite refuses that sense of the given. This refusal occurs as a result of the recreation of another urban terrain. However, it is not just the recreation of the given. More significantly it is the creation from the given of connections, divisions, spaces, etc., that could only have come into existence because of the parasite's productive presence. (It should be remembered that the parasite frays; it neither adds nor ornaments.) The parasite creates. It does so by undoing and transforming—thus fraying—the edges, lines, borders of an original setting. A procedure which, as has already been argued, is itself only possible because the urban has been reconfigured, within Goodwin's detailed study and creation of projects, as that which occasions and allows for transformation. Fraying cannot have a limit because what frays are limits.

THERE IN THE VANISHING
Notes on Elizabeth Presa's Moon Water

There in the vanishing. Not there however, as a trace of a mark left once, as though it were a mere imprint. What is left once may announce no more than a simple passage. The mark of an immediate moment. Left once. Imprints that mark the singular moment will start to gather other elements to them. They come to be filled such that what is there is not the vanishing but an absence having been replaced. Filled in, literally. Vanishing however, is something else. What is there, there in the vanishing, has a different status, a different quality and as such its relationship to presentation is significantly altered. Any approach to this different quality has to begin with vanishing. (As a beginning the ostensible concern of this sculptural work—*Moon Water*—is vanishing.) Not with absence as though a melancholic hold takes over the question of presentation. In addition, any concern with vanishing cannot be restricted by a posited return to forms of plenitude, as though vanishing gestures at its being overcome. An overcoming linked as much to a philosophy of art as to a conception of the work of art. The possibilities—absence and presence—are unable to define vanishing. It was of course this very supposition that has already been registered by holding to the possibility that what there is, is there in the vanishing.

If there is a way into this possibility then it does not lie in reworking the interplay of absence and presence. Rather, the possibility lies in the formulation itself. As a beginning there is the following question—how is the relationship between 'there' and 'vanishing' to be understood? (The question for art is if course how is that relation to be presented?) Answering both—the first a discursive claim while the second brings the ineliminable presence of material into play—starts with the recognition that 'vanishing' marks process. Once centrality is given to process this allows the question of vanishing to take on different forms. What needs to be taken up is what it would mean not just for there to be that which is there in the vanishing—even if the process is understood as resulting in the state of 'having vanished'—the significant question, now, is how does the process—the process of vanishing, one holding in play a 'there is' quality—allow for presentation and thus art's work?

Questions should not summon the work of art. Were this to be the case then any philosophical concern with art's work would be reduced to the latter's inclusion as mere example. If there is a demand to be made then its register is different. Art's work makes demands. Responding is to act responsibly. Enacting a responsibility to art. At the same time, of course, such a response is itself that which is responsible for art.

At work here—a work whose description must note the presence of photographs, mirrors and sculptural form—is a project defined by a sense of passage. No matter how that sense is understood—and in this instance 'passage' can signal the movement to form as much as any more specific and thus individualized sense—the work's most demanding quality is the nature of the relationship it envisages to sculpture's own relation to the interplay of materiality and form. An interplay always realized in terms of a becoming determinant. And yet, it is not as though there is a single question that can define sculpture's relation to form creation. The history of sculpture could be formulated such that it divides as much between a concern with ostensible subject matter (i.e. with the work's meaning) as between one defined by the differing ways form creation occurs. Any concern with form that grounds it in the use of materials while at the same time linking it to the process of becoming form begins to define the sculptural beyond the hold of idealism. The effect of idealism is that it either precludes a concern with matter (often by repositioning it in terms of matter's idealization), or which subjugates form such that it is then taken to be no more than the expression of a dominant Idea. The sculptural elements in *Moon Water* operate in a radically different way. Their break with idealism can be located in the way material presence—form—is created. The process by which jellyfish covered in plaster registers a presence does not occur by providing the form as though all that is at work is their imprint. The contrary is the case. Form emerges, as does the luminescent coating given to the individual works, with their vanishing. Form occurs—it should be possible to begin to establish a relationship between process and form as an event—as a result of vanishing.

Who then creates? The question of creativity is not intended to open up the problem of intentionality. It is clear that Elizabeth Presa's hand is at work. Rather, what is raised by the question of creation is the temporal direction of form creation. That temporality is also played out in the other elements that comprise the installation. The inclusion of mirrors whose tain has faded to such a point that the visual and temporal immediacy demanded by the operation of the mirror is no longer operative, also works to complicate time. What becomes complicated is the possibility that the immediacy, which comes to have its correlate in an understanding of a simple continuity of construction, constitutes, perhaps constructs, the work. Rather than the sculpture appearing from stone, wood, etc., where the material is the point of origination that is in some sense prior to sculptural presence even if it is retained as part of that presence such that there is an apparent slide from matter to its sculptured form—a sculptural gesture that literalizes matter by trapping it within a logic of production structured by temporal continuity—with the constitutive elements of *Moon Water* form emerges neither from extension nor contraction but from vanishing.

Vanishing has at least two registers. In the first instance it is inextricably bound up with the way the plaster and gauze models acquire form and take on texture. Linked to this register are the mirrors whose power of reflection is retained in the tain's vanishing. Vanishing registers a trace precisely because it is a process. Processes admit of degrees. Vanishing is linked to a logic of production as much as it is to material presence. The other register is equally concerned with the presence of matter. Nonetheless, vanishing is now more directly concerned with the relationship between matter and time. Time not, however, as the abstract quality within which matter can be both said to exist and thus experienced. The temporality in question is the operation of time as part of matter's work and therefore as part of the work of art. Rather, than occurring in time, the temporality of the object is integral to the operative quality of a work. What this means is that the relationship between time and matter—the temporality of a material presence defined by vanishing—is articulated within the object's presentation. Presentation is not defined by the simple existence of an object. What is of concern is the presentation of art work.

Presentation, or more accurately the event of form, is that which becomes determinant—becoming through vanishing. Locating this process within material, delimiting it therefore in terms of an account of matter's becoming present, is to allow the object's material presence to be positioned beyond the hold of immediacy. Immediacy, understood as a temporal term identifies a specific moment. That which occurs immediately can be understood as taking place in the 'now' of its happening. What occurs does so immediately. Immediacy and vanishing—punctum and process—cannot be assimilated to each other. Moreover, vanishing is not a moment within a process. The elements that comprise *Moon Water* hold out against immediacy. They do so through the event of form.

Matter and time are given a different configuration. Once the object's presence is taken into consideration—and this is a consideration whose quality acquires a necessary insistence because of the nature of an installation—then what is being presented is the process by the which the object becomes form. Here an array of objects is present. With their presence there is the event of form. Form occurs because vanishing is allowed to work and thus to become the work. What is there is so, as the vanishing.

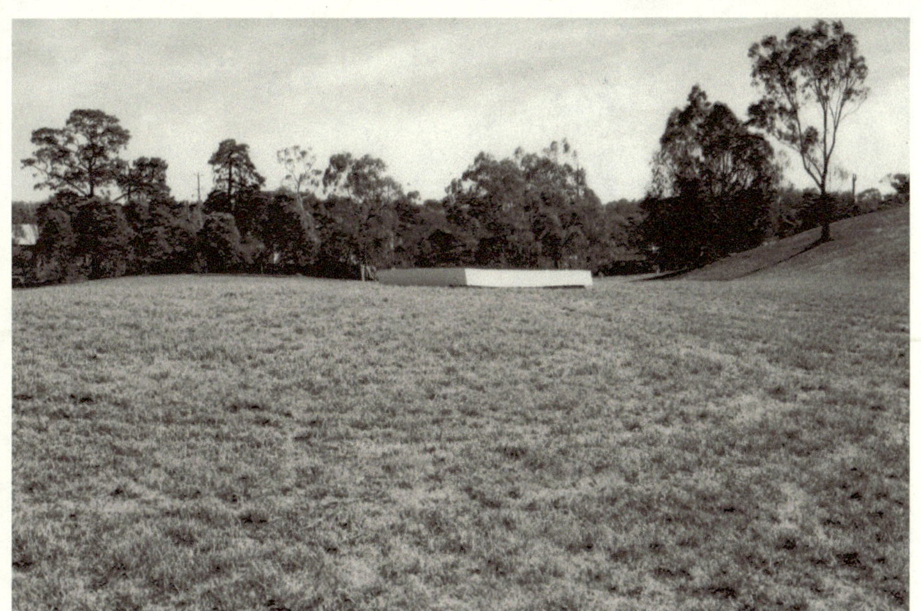

32. Terri Bird, *Recycling Fictions of Being*, recycled plastic panels, 2002.

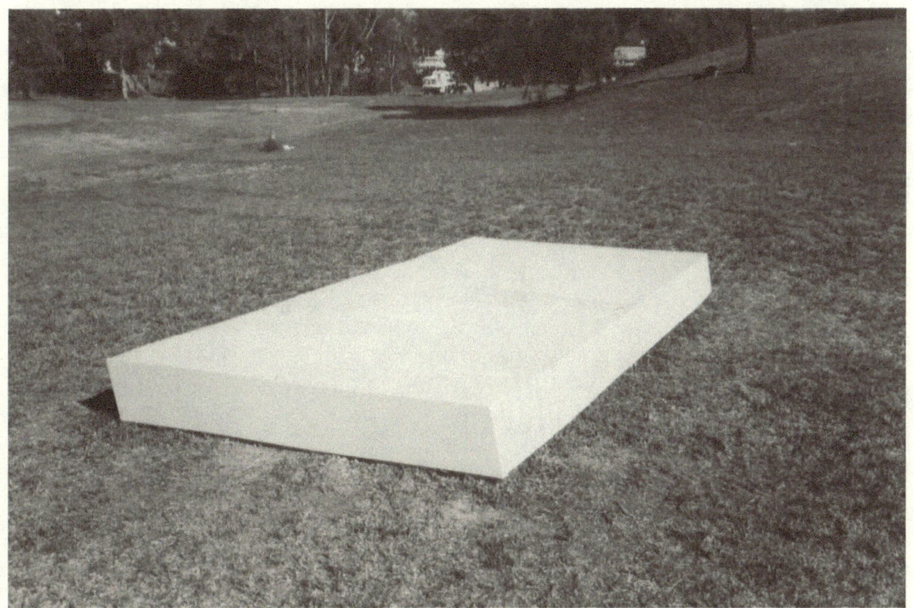

33. Terri Bird, *Recycling Fictions of Being*, recycled plastic panels, 2002.

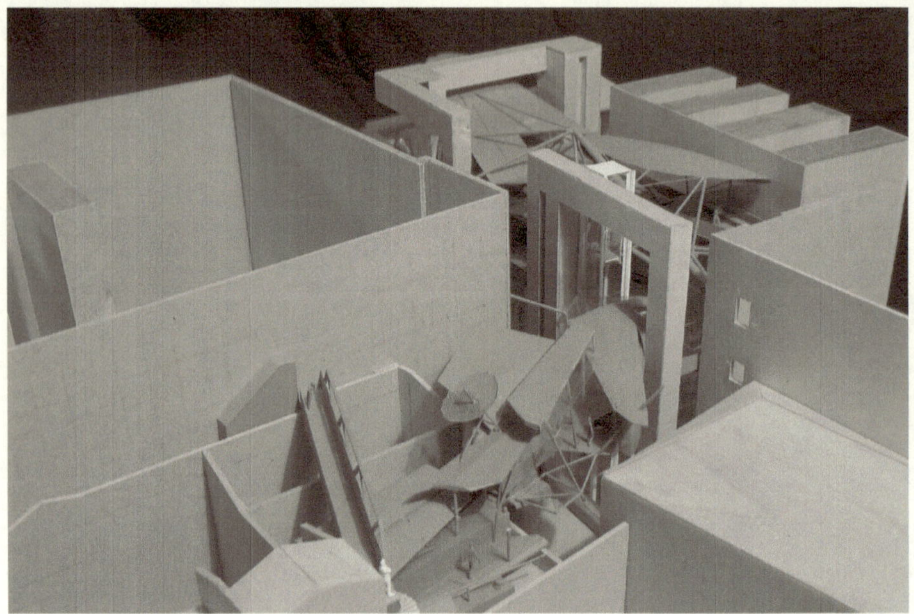

34. Richard Goodwin, *Parasite Actions: Monkey Model 06.*

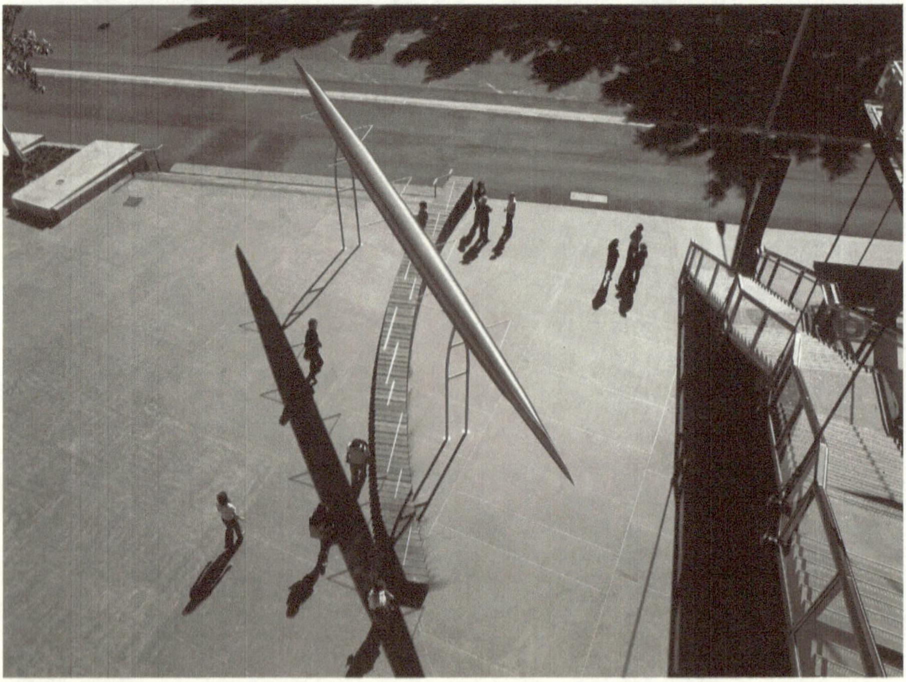

35. Richard Goodwin, *Bond Street Parasite.*

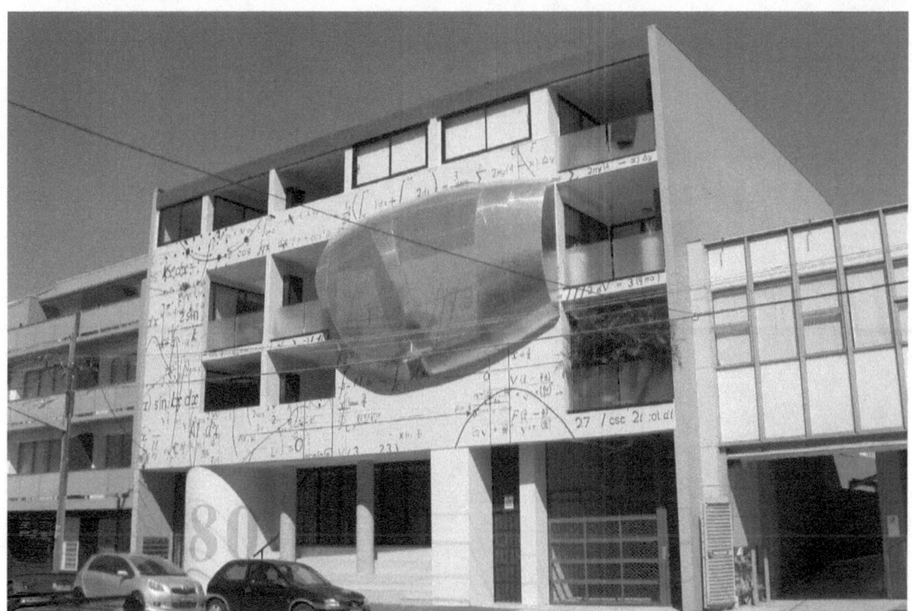

36. Richard Goodwin, *Parasite Façade in Cope St Alexandria*.

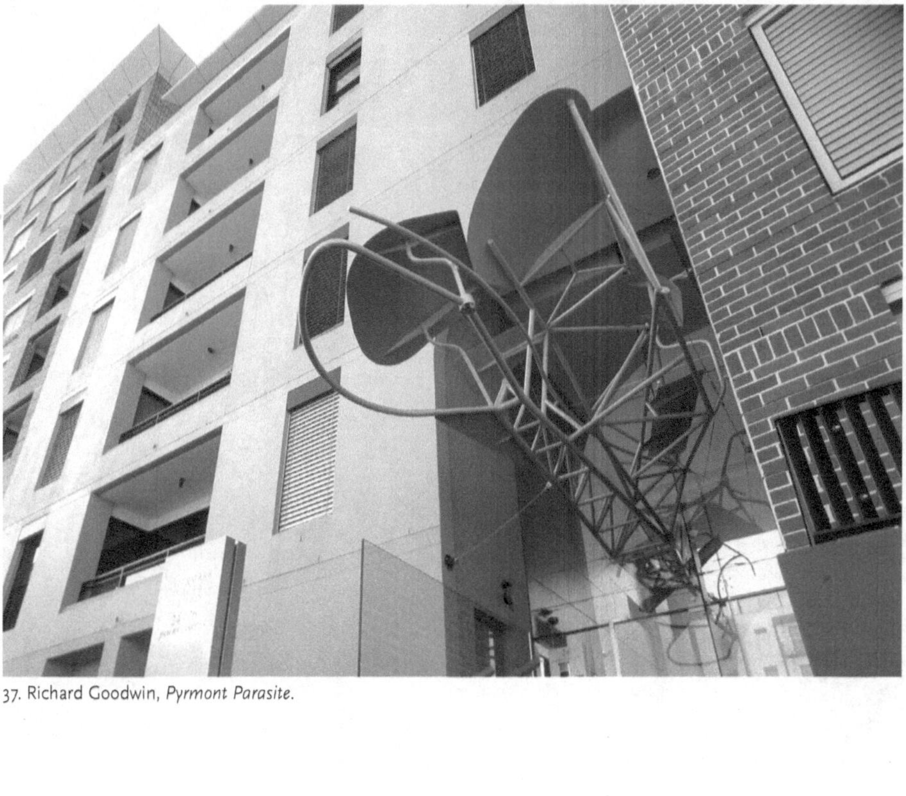

37. Richard Goodwin, *Pyrmont Parasite*.

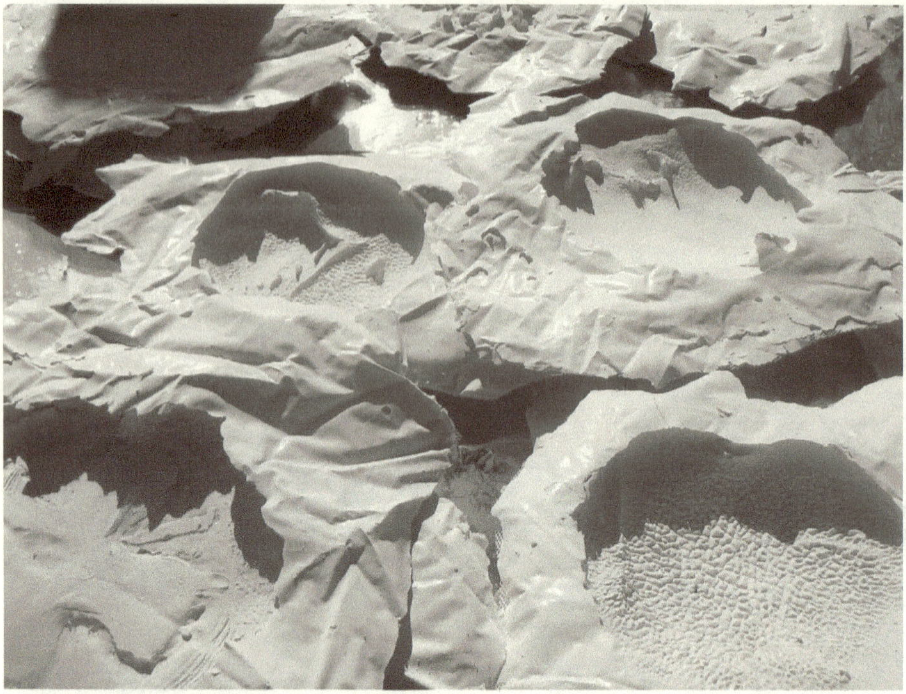

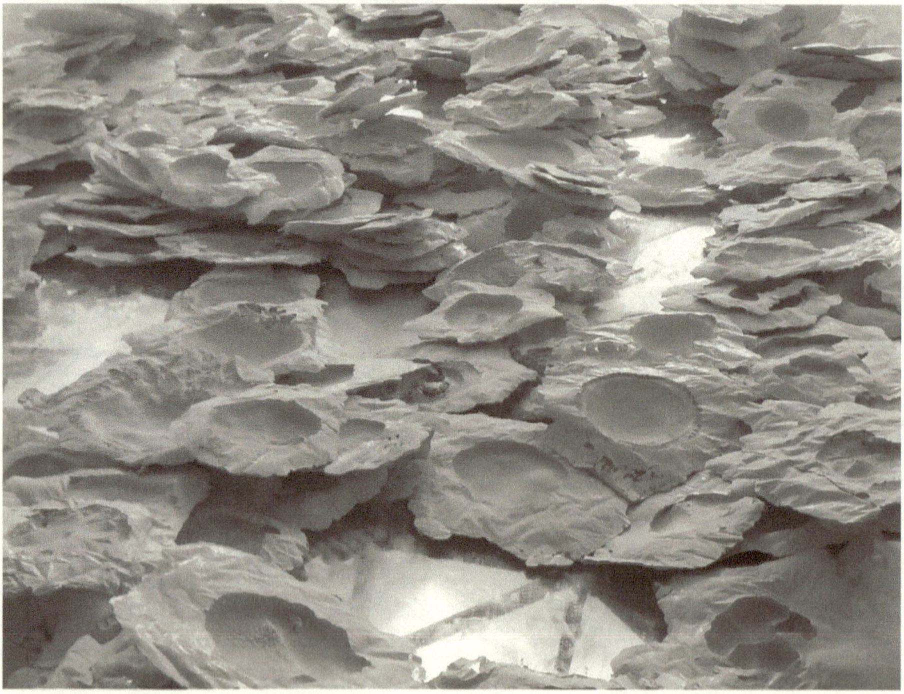

38-39. Elizabeth Presa, *Moon Water*, Jelly fish, plaster, gauze, salt water, mirrors, 8m x 9m, 2005.

WRITING

SEEING FLORENCE

What is Florence's name? What is named by Florence? These question point to the complex relationship that pertains between translation and place in the first instance and then experience and place in the second. Moreover, the question of experience is already mediated by an economy of images that provides any original experience—the often craved first experience—with a sense of déjà vu. The question remains, is it possible to begin either writing or experience with the words, 'What I see, what I see.' (As Joseph Roth did his 1921 essay on walking.) And then continue with a description. As if seeing and reporting were simply there. Both having the status of unclouded and unproblematic activities. Seeing and describing working together in the creation of an experiential mapping of the seen. The city woven within sight and description. If anything were to check this slide from view to words then it would be the already present intrusion of the image into experience itself.

In his famous story *A Little Ramble*, the title here is all, Robert Walser finished with these words: 'I encountered a few carts, otherwise nothing, and I had seen some children on the highway. We don't need to see anything out of the ordinary. We already see so much'. Walser wrote this words in 1914. Prior to the First World War and thus prior to the moment in which experience would begin to be accompanied not just by images but images that had the same timed sequence as experience. Moreover, they were on public display. The horror of the war and its effect on experience cannot be separated from its re-presentation, at the time, and then subsequently, within images. Images not only took the place of experience they allowed for it. Walser's words today are simply naïve. What has happened both to experience as well as to the pervasive hold of images means that despite the desire for both simplicity and originality, neither is possible. We have simply seen too much.

And yet a longing is harboured. Something could remain. There may be a reality, part of city, a view, a corner caught at sunset, holding open in the moments of its passing a remnant of experience that no matter how fleeting might be thought to be authentic. What is longed for is that which has as not already been either transformed or consumed. A longing already dashed in advance.

~

From the Duomo to San Lorenzo is a short walk. The approach via Borgo San Lorenzo takes minutes. As for the Chapel, Manetti finishing Brunelleschi's original plans allows a thought of the Duomo to be carried down one street prior to an opening in which the organization of space has a type of familiarity. Proceeding from the Church through Palazzo Mannelli-Ricardi, it is again a short distance to the market: the Mercato Centrale. The impressive nineteenth century building designed by Mengoni and built in 1874 was a place that defined the city's internal life. The importation of food, its consumption and then exportation as waste chart the history of any city. As a complex cycle of activity it accompanies the city's political and cultural development. Moreover, noting the transformation of the market is to note the city's transformation. What occurs is neither intentional nor planned.

To the extent that the name Florence names a set of possible experiences, some of which will have already occurred prior to any entry into the city, (this will, of course, be true for any of the names that Florence has) the continual multiplication of the name keeps returning in forms of singular events. The market continues to refer to a past in which the provision of meat, fish, fruit and vegetables kept the market open as a popular site. As times changed different economies were at work. What marks that change is not the market, it remains open, but the reorientation of the popular. In lieu of a conception of the popular defined by residents and internal needs, there is a conception in which the dependence of the internal economy on tourists and thus on the provision of a service industry has meant a transformation in what the market sells. There are still remnants of the market that still serve the residential population. Stalls that are a reminder of that other sense of the popular. While the supermarket usurps the market, the Mercato Centrale begins to sell more ornate forms of pasta. The olive oil is ready packaged for a trip back to Baltimore or Kyoto rather than to the Borgo Pinti.

~

The packaging of Florence, of its 'treasures' and thus of that which has been left behind and from which a certain present is created have been taken over by a version of the international. It is as though whatever Florence may be it is 'our' concern. There is of course a truth in this. Restoration and conservation are not done for the inhabitants. Such projects are done for 'us'. Conservation's prevailing ideology is that what is conserved is the work's eternal quality. The eternal has been saved to sure up a specific naming. The naming in which were it not for 'us' our Florence would have been lost. While outside, this 'us' grants itself the status of an authentic concern with Florence, a concern not thought to be evidenced necessarily by the Florentines themselves.

The whir of cameras and voices, groups assemble and are then held after the simulated click of the digital camera marks the image's creation. Image upon image, groups created to be displayed. Equally, art, no longer a silent site of contemplation, let alone the locus of discovery, provides the points that define groups. Places of visit and instruction create and recreate images of Florence that are folded into the visit. Folding into it and beginning to define the city since they will have already provided it with its measure. Post cards and photos capture sculptures and painting. They are all reduced to a manageable size such that material presence will have been subdued and whatever chance a work may have had to overwhelm, will have already been expunged with the image's creation. Experience, to the extent that it accepts the already given, has become unthinkable without an accompanying image. And yet, precisely because of the memory that material presence occasions—think of Cellini's Perseus in the Loggia dei Lanzi—the image will always disappoint. Materiality can only give rise to a form of melancholia.

~

The railways station—Statzione di Santa Maria Novella—designed by the Gruppo Toscano stages the complex relationship between modernism and fascism. Not only was the orginal design for the station approved by Mussolini, Florence's Jews were deported from it. Today, as leading members of Italy's ruling elite revisit that past in order to mute its complications—fascists become patriots—Florence continues to be visited by those for whom history remains uncertain. While it is possible to experience the station as no more than a site of entry the question of its past effaced by its meld into Florence as an already experienced event created and recreated through images, there is the possibility that this other presence will be able to insist. If this were to occur it would involve the possibility of another mark and thus another naming.

~

Experience is always limited by expectation. Expectation has its contemporary form in images that allow for while they accompany experience. The name 'Florence' consist therefore of that structure of expectation. Expectation means that there is an already present form of knowledge. 'We' know how to experience Florence. What has already occurred will continue. It is of course at this precise point that there is an opening. The opening does not reveal the authentic as opposed to the already present. It is not as though there are actual moments that have been kept away and remain the true vestiges of an authentic past. What counters the structure of expectation is not the authentic but that which undoes the structure itself. Moments, marks, signs even events that refuse the setting of the already experienced. While they need not be remarkable in themselves what they introduce are forms incredulity. Aesthetic moments that charge sites whilst diminishing the hold of others. An introduction of a political sensibility that reintroduces the complex interplay of power and the present by charging the present in a way that refuses the blanketing effect of an already experienced and thus already deadened now. The result would be that 'we' no longer knew. In not knowing, Florence would begin to name other possibilities. While such a description might obtain for all cities the way this possibility occurs will always be specific. It may be therefore that seeing, perhaps writing, would flow from this not knowing.

PLACE

* Place while given is never just given. More is in place. More will have always been in place.

* Writing about a place—any place—will necessitate that the place be identified, that it be located and thus that it be placed. Each of these moments is an activity; identifying, placing, locating. As activities, as that which is undertaken, they bring with them the ineliminable mark of mediation. How then is this mediation to be understood? What would be involved in any attempt to position locating, placing, identifying? The question of positioning as with that of understanding are made more difficult by the fact that the activities are thought either to have been spontaneous or simply to work with the given. Mediation is denied by the feint of innocence. Once this position is shown to harbour a complexity that will belie any innocence—rendering that innocence merely putative—how *then* are these acts to be understood?

* If there is change, if moving from one to the other—from innocence to complexity—is not a just a moving forward but a moving back allowing for a possible future what will the time of this movement be? What type of work will have been undertaken?

* With the question—and this will be true of questioning as an activity—what is brought to bear upon that activity is the actual process that it seeks to identify. Not the answer but the process/activity itself. What is the place of questioning? What is placed by it?

* Even with the question place insists.

* Developing place must be specific; sites will always be specific. And yet specificity is not just the evocation of this place, the positing of an already given geography; this place as opposed to that place. Specificity pertains to that which will always be involved in the thinking of place, of the location of a site. What comes to be given are the predetermined sites of meaning; corner, room, building, street, city, region, nation.

* With the given—the predetermined present—there are the necessary and important imposition of relations. Positions captured and held by the play of prepositions; in, by, between, with, etc. Part of that play will be an already present implication; one will always be with another.

* What is it to question the given? What is the place of such a questioning? Answering will hinge on the gift and the work of its inexorable logic. With the gift and its impossible refusal the temporality of tradition is brought into play.

* Here in lieu of place as simple, place will need to be taken with its necessary interconnection with space. What is at work with the incorporation of space cannot be accounted for in terms of a simple addition. Space has not been added on. It is neither emblem nor ornament but brings with it the attempt—albeit a halting initial attempt—to signal the already present work of complexity.

* With complexity there will be the question of its own understanding. What will it mean to open up complexity? What will have been there?

* Once complexity comes to insist as a question then the answers that are already given will begin to lose their hold. What had been held in place prior to the opening allowed by the question is the incorporation of complexity into a schema that locate it in opposition to the simple (the axiom, the simple particular, etc.) such that the specificity of complexity lay in its being an amalgam of simples. Complexity became no more than the consequence of the process of addition. Process here will be a simple movement that admits of regress. The supposition would be therefore that complexity can be reduced to it founding simples. What had been built is able to be broken down and then rebuilt. At work within this already

structured presence is the possibility of a simple beginning. Here simplicity will take on the guise of innocence and, as with innocence, what will have been disguised is the insistent presence of a founding complexity; in other words a set up that is *ab initio* complex.

* Complexity will have started to admit of its own founding complexity.

* The interplay of space and place will have to allow for a complex geography. Once geography has to maintain complexity then the standard place allocated to geometry may have to change. With it time will have to be reworked. The temporality of progress and regress will no longer pertain—other time holds sway.

* With any jumble of possibilities speed—the nature of speed, the right of speed—must be taken up. Movement from one position to the next; abandoning one understanding to take up another; undoing a specific link to allow for another, all these undertakings—undertakings that bring with them an inevitable necessity, especially in their formulation—cannot just happen. Positing brings with it an inescapable foundering.

* Allowing for speed—the right speed coupled to the actual possibility of movement—returns insisting considerations.

* With speed, with the possibility of the orchestration of a movement the inherent complexity—its inhering as an originally present—will emerge.

* What is there, will have been there, is the site of an intrusion. The intruder is neither enemy nor friend. Intrusion marks the presence of a primordial relation that will always defy simplicity.

* Who intrudes? Whose intruder? What is it to live with intrusion?

* Intrusion places the gift. The gift intrudes. Intrusion cannot be refused. With this presence there is more than one. And yet there cannot be just two. At work here is that which exceeds addition.

* Intruding by becoming the given creates place. The more than

one that was always more than one will come to define the nature of place. Being more it allows for relation. In allowing it, it spaces.

* Spacing becomes the site of the more than one.

ON/WITHIN

* On what will it be written? Within what domain and thus what place will that which is written give itself over to an understanding; as a gift even to its own understanding? A self-giving opening opened up by refusing the possibility of any original singularity. Denying by re-fusing it a place (in place) and thus allowing for another fusing. Another place turning the singular back upon itself and with it inscribing it in a complexity from which it cannot hold itself apart since it will always have been a part of it. Within the inseparability of apart/a part there is that which grounds any singularity. The singularity is the other gift, always given *après coup*.

* Within this opening there are questions and positions that turn around the temporal distinction between singularity and plurality. In holding the distinction as temporal and thus allowing existence (maintained as a differential ontology), this holding as allowing opens up the surface by demanding that it be given another depth.

* Within it, on it, it is given space and thus a place however both take place in time. The time in question is not an addition. It does not add to existence as though it were present as a mere ornament. Time inheres in any thought of existence and with any instantiation. Presence does not just occur in time, presence is as the occurrence of time. Time's presentation. What will have to be retained—maintained throughout—is the already complex nature of any presentation. In retaining what must be held open is the difficulty of thinking this complexity.

* Within writing, within its initial presentation, a reductive and simple presentation, writing could be taken as being that which

is placed on. With it therefore there is that taking and placing that tradition has for writing. Held for it. Writing as always writing on. On internality, a topi; an already existent place for its occurrence. The latter is that on which the writing is. Its being—the 'is'—leads writing to the surface and thus as only ever superficial; of the surface, *superficies superficialis.*

* Within writing what emerges is the place of its own enactment. With what is maintained, within it though not reducible to it, is the language of surface and depth, of form and function, of information and poetry, of statement and ornament, etc. What is held up, buttressed, therefore is the site of a language of construction and effectuation. In thinking through this site what will arise within it is the ineliminable presence of conflict; the conflicting logics of construction. They are written with a writing that will bear out conflict's primordality and as such these writings demand a thinking of both construction and effectuation which in resisting the attribution of the essence (*Wesen*)—and with it essential thinking, even a putative redemption of the essence—necessitates taking up these conflicting possibilities. In distancing the essence, in holding to conflict, a politics of construction—a construction that will still allow for writing as itself conflictual—comes to be housed.

* On the writing there will always turn another type of adventure, a different eventuality, another coming-to-be, which itself will already have turned back upon itself, thereby turning back any simple 'itself' thus causing that change that alters the becoming and which left it—the writing—no longer an inscription. Neither on it, nor with it, this not really within it, but as it, as writing itself; the primordially present active within substance.

* On a turning, which, in already being present, affirms the ineliminable necessity and with it the anoriginal presence of doubling there must be another writing. Its possibility demanding another alterity. Demanding equally to be built upon.

* On and within a writing coming to its own by being a complex inscription—inscribing time within space, holding spaced time—that in being the only hold of any singularity, is at the same time the only possible place of its inscription. Singularity's own

opening. Writing's own—that to which writing must own up—is a plurality and thus a complexity that can never be disowned.

* Within this writing the extending range of time must continue to be noted, noting thereby the already present inscription. Time remains always figuring within any productive logic.

* On time what will always remain to be added is that any addition will demand to be thought within that construal of addition as complexity where the later demands to be understood as what has already been subject to—here the subject of—that which the term names. What will always need to be taken up, therefore, is complexity's own complexity.

* Within any given term, any apparent simplicity must figure an original complexity. An already present complexity prior either to addition or singularity.

* On the surface there will not have been any addition since the surface, in being recast, is no longer a simple face on which inscriptions, additions, supplements, etc., are placed, in order then to be taken as an adjunct; a joining marked out as secondary. With the dispersal of the surface another logic is demanded, enacted within a different production. The difficulty is that any dispersal of the traditional presentation of the surface and therefore of writing as that which figures on surfaces, in part declaring them to be surfaces, is that it will have to maintain, again at the same time, what is given, and therefore what is presented as marking out the surface, what marks it is the presence of a face, a sur-face.

* Within time, thus at the moment that the surface is taken as effaced it must also, at the same time—a time already complex because of its harboured and maintained plurality—occasion that doubling that moves the simple oppositions between surface and depth or writing and content back from the posited—thus traditional—centrality. Again the same that resists any reduction to itself. Marking thereby the abeyance of the same-as-itself.

* On what is given by tradition—a gift that will always already have been given—it will never be a question of either subtraction (denial, disavowal, repression, etc.). Refusing is always a form of

acceptance. Change as alteration cannot but maintain a repetition of the Same. Ornamentation will involve another setting and thus its incorporation into a different logic.

* On, once taken as a designated setting, on here rather than there and thus, as 'on' being the apparent provision of any setting, it follows that the word 'on' will itself therefore have to be taken as presupposing a site, or as a positioning prior either to another positioning or another placing. With these possibilities it—'on'—marks out a type of pre-position that is already positioned. This complex site working within that complex disavowing reduction positions it as the site on which there is writing, on which there is ornamentation, on which the decoration.

* On within doubles, since within what is marked out as being 'on', or indeed of being 'in', there will be the automatic effacing of a reduction that holds the distinction between surface and depth in place. Replacing becomes a form of repetition that holds open the possibility of a redemption working beyond the dominance of the same.

* On any surface there is a decoration. Even if it were functional any ornament is to be found on the building. And yet the question that must endure, the one that is still left is the relation between this on and that which takes place within? With this question writing and the surface, with their designations given by their own traditional formulations can be taken to occupy the same space. Occupying it at the same time. As such the same open and reopens—opening any positing of an initial and singular time—allowing in the opening an instantiation with which the same is no longer able to remain the same as its self. (It is of course that this position was always there, present as a potentiality.) There has to be therefore another possibility for the same. A possibility that cannot be the same.

* On, taken as that which brings the surface and in bringing it brings depth will find its position incorporated within a logic that always works within and in so doing generates the surface, etc. On will have ceded its place to within. In giving that place away it will come to be repositioned. What will never be lost is the possibility of holding on. And yet with it, in holding on, it must be positioned

beyond its place within the oppositions that cannot be held on and thus can no longer be allowed to hold.

* On figures within, with in. Harboured within another logic. Not the logic that is to be taken as working within—if that is taken to be simple opposition to the surface—it is rather another logic one working within, working the within; in other words that which comprises within's work.

* On the end, no matter how arbitrary, what can never be eliminated is its future enactment, another repetition. Repeating on.

* On repetition what can never be excluded is a finality marked out as on the end.

* On however, that which is marked out as being on, can only be maintained if it is incorporated within that logic—within's work—in which it will emerge as the always present singular. A singular that is necessarily secondary and in being secondary is secured as part of that logic that in taking place within constructs the whole.

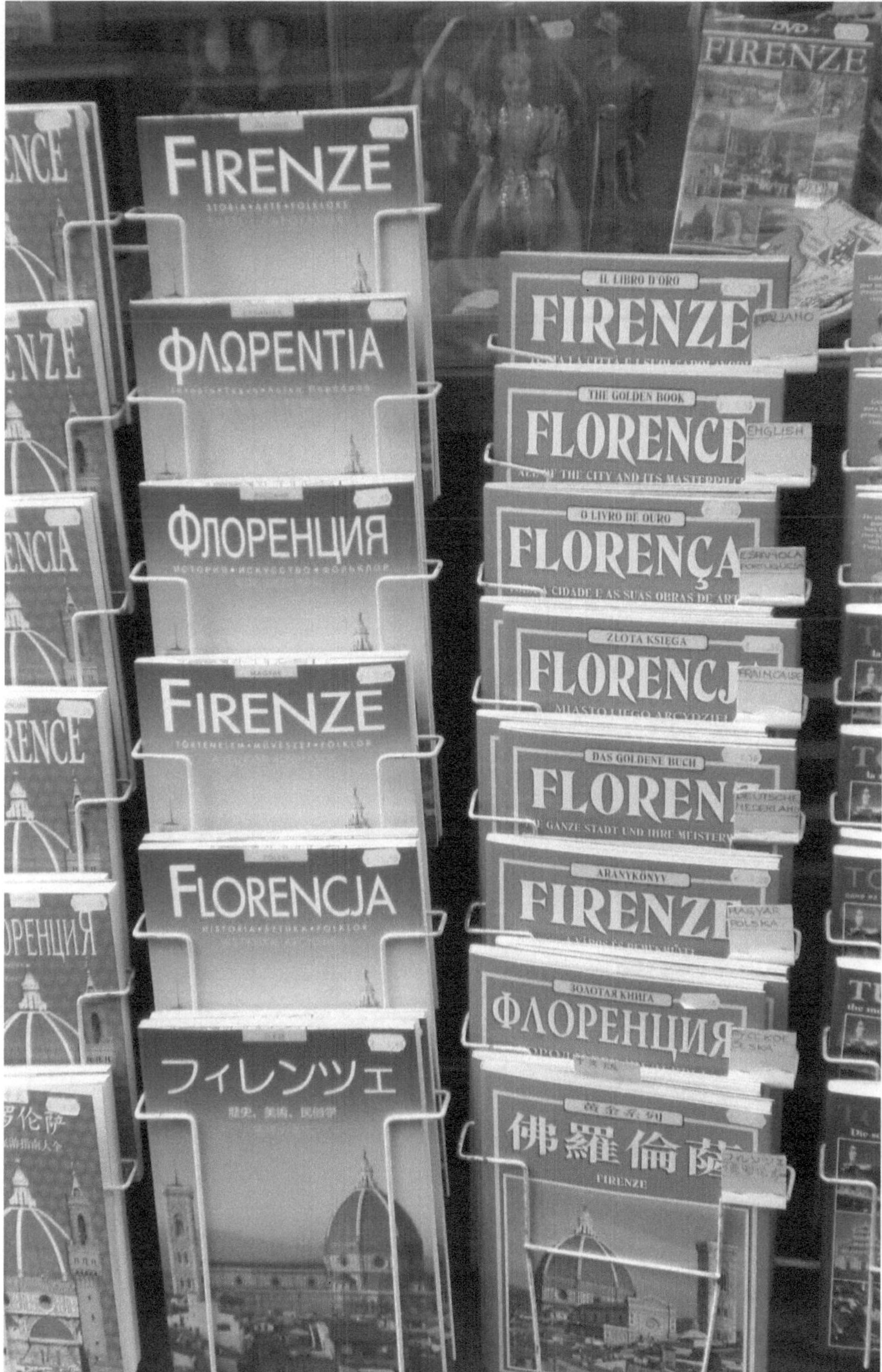

40. Andrew Benjamin, *Seeing Florence 1*, 2008.

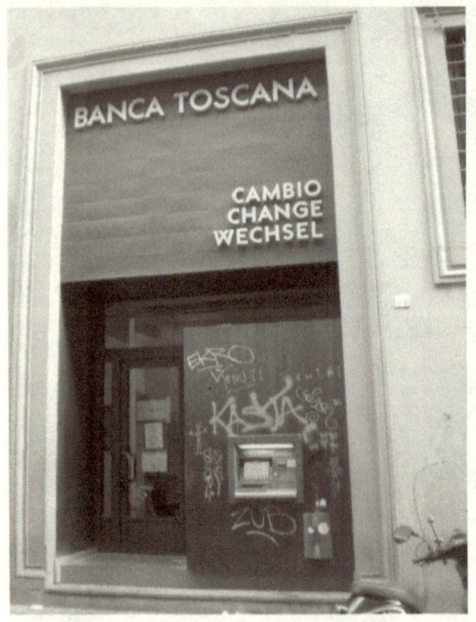

41. Andrew Benjamin, *Seeing Florence 2*, 2008.

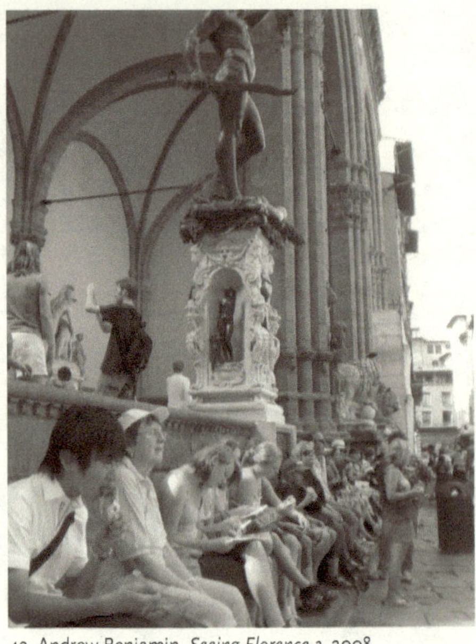

42. Andrew Benjamin, *Seeing Florence 3*, 2008.

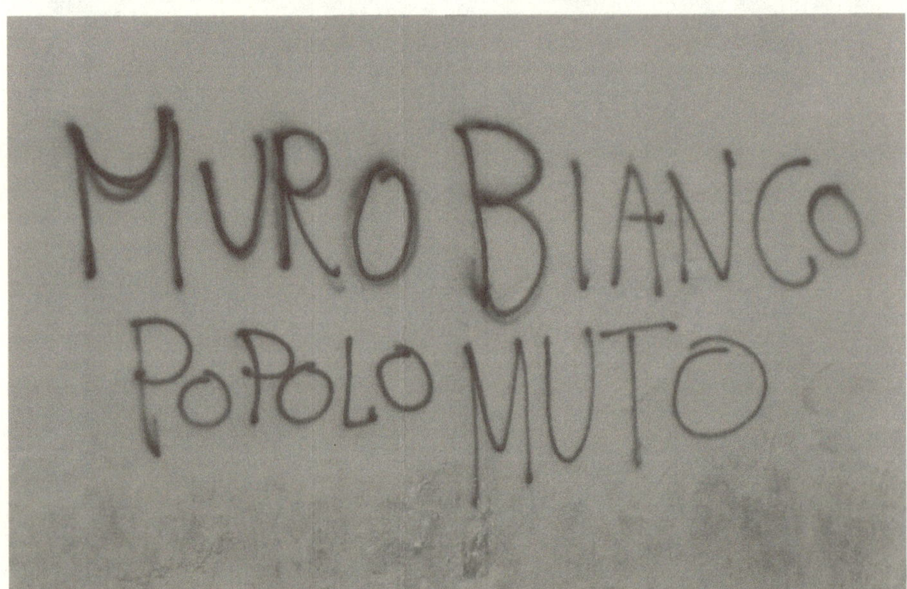

43. Andrew Benjamin, *Seeing Florence 4*, 2008.

www.ingramcontent.com/pod-product-compliance
Lightning Source LLC
LaVergne TN
LVHW090946080826
845145LV00003B/913

* 9 7 8 0 9 8 0 8 1 9 7 0 0 *